Christ's Way

to

RESTORATION

Books by Philip G. Samaan

Christ's Way to Pray
Christ's Way to Spiritual Growth
Christ's Way of Reaching People
Christ's Way of Making Disciples
Portraits of the Messiah
Blood Brothers

To order: Call (423) 236-2982 - (706) 935-8800
E-mail: pgs@southern.edu

Christ's Way
to
RESTORATION

Philip G. Samaan

The author assumes full responsibility for the accuracy of all facts and quotations as cited in this book.

Unless otherwise indicated, Bible texts in this book are from the *New King James Version*. Copyright © 1979, 1980, 1982 by Thomas Nelson, Inc. Used by permission. All rights reserved.

Cover designed by Philip Mills
Cover illustration by Brian Dunne
Typeset: 12/14.4 Adobe Garamond Pro

PRINTED IN U.S.A.

13   12   11   10   09   5   4   3   2   1

ISBN 978-0-9824395-0-0

Printed by Review and Herald Graphics.

Dedication

Dedicated to my wife Sherilyn
whose implicit trust in Christ inspired this book.

Contents

Introduction

I don't know about you, but I do not like watching the news or reading about it anymore. I am totally turned off by so much horror, mayhem, and wanton violence. How do we begin to make any sense out of the abduction, molestation, and cold-blooded murder of an innocent little girl! How do we begin to comprehend it when a bunch of teenagers gang up on one of their own classmates and split her skull with baseball bats! No real explanation from any of this can be found, except as we look at the mystery of iniquity alluded to in God's word. Lucifer conceived iniquity in his heart, birthed it and fashioned it into a full-blown rebellion against his Maker.

In this book, we will try to explore this mystery of iniquity, and to trace the anatomy of rebellion in the heart of the one closest to God's heart. We will consider how this malignant spirit of rebelliousness in Lucifer's heart infected our first parents, and was insidiously transmitted to all of their descendants. Without Christ's plan of redemption from the foundation of the world, we would all be doomed to suffer eternal death. But

1

in His eternal and self-sacrificing love to save us from ourselves, the Son of God offered Himself on the cross as our Substitute and Surety. He also planted His divine enmity in the human heart as a defense against evil, giving us the freedom and incentive to decide for the right.

Although, He granted us free choice, His ardent desire for us is to make the right choice of trusting and obeying Him. The root reason *par excellence* as to why Christ came to die for us is to save us from our sin, and to deliver us from certain death. Thus He may draw us to love Him with all our hearts, and to love and live His commandments, reflecting His character. Such love, trust, and obedience towards Christ and His ways safeguard us against self-centeredness and rebelliousness. Considering all what Christ's love has done for us, wouldn't we want to love Him, lean on Him, live for Him? Wouldn't we want being like Him to be our highest and holiest ambition? For by choosing Him, we choose life, abundant here and glorious in heaven.

The key to our restoration from rebellion is Christ's awesome sacrifice. However, there are different humanistic conjectures inferred as to why Jesus died on the cross. Some think it was primarily to give us freedom of choice, to demonstrate to us His love, or to set for us an example to follow. Others explain that Jesus died to shower His abundant grace upon us and to grant us unconditional redemption. Still others argue that Jesus shed His blood to set us free from obedience to the law of God, and to liberate us from striving to live a victorious Christian life.

However, the Bible is abundantly clear about the indispensable and primary reason why Jesus came to our sinful world to die. He came to save us from our sins, and to give us the abundant and eternal life. He came to honor His immutable law of

Introduction

love by illustrating how justice and mercy kissed each other. All of this was to propel us to walk with Jesus, become like Him, and prepare us to become citizens of Heaven. Christ indeed came to enable us to move away from our rebellion and move toward His restoration.

Our freedom of choice is vital to the plan of salvation, and it was there since the beginning of creation. It was there before the cross when God created the holy angels, unfallen beings, and our first parents. He made Himself vulnerable by voluntarily creating all with free will. Yet He would not have it any other way, because His divine love calls for loving reciprocity and harmonious cooperation. The first Adam abused this privilege by making the wrong choice, but Christ, the Second Adam, made the right choice by living God's love and obeying His law before the fallen and unfallen worlds. He died the death we deserved, choosing to honor God and His immutable law. Thus, by His grace we may deliberately and diligently make the right choices in life.

Christ's shed blood cries out to us from the stained soil of Calvary: make the right choice, walk with Me in love and obedience! God ardently desires us to enter the victorious experience of the Second Adam by not making the wrong choices. Although the risk is there that we may abuse our freedom of choice, He constantly urges us not to do so. But if we make the wrong choice and repent, we have an Advocate with the Father, who graciously provides us with a way of escape.

The apostle John affirms why Jesus died on the cross when he writes that the "blood of Jesus cleanses us from all sin" (1 Jn. 1:7). This inspired word is to exhort us *not* to choose to sin; but if we make the wrong choice and sin, we have an Advocate with the Father (2:1). Although God offers us hope, we should not presume upon His grace and use it as a license to sin. God's definite plan for us, as we make our crucial decisions, is to abide in Christ and to "walk just as He walked" (2:6). We purpose in our hearts to walk with Him and live for Him, a selfless life of total submission to His will not ours.

My dear reader, let us prayerfully heed this appeal: Many presume on God's mercy by carelessly choosing to sin. There are too many wrong choices made today, so why not determine to make the right choices to trust and obey Jesus? Choices are so vitally crucial in determining our destiny here and the hereafter. Why not abandon our self-centered and humanistic choices, and adopt Christ-centered and biblical choices? Why not choose to faithfully walk with Jesus in this world that we may continue walking with Him in glory? Why not ask Him to help us fulfill the reason why He came to die–His salvation from our sins, His restoration from our rebellion?

CHAPTER ONE

Free Choice But Right Choice

One day a bright student walked into my office to "discuss" an important decision he was about to make. As he shared his experience with me that morning, I sensed that he had already made up his mind. He just needed my sympathy and support for his decision. He wanted me to say something encouraging to help him feel supported about the wrong life choice he had already made. His decision was clearly not according to the counsel of God's word, nevertheless he felt convicted that he was being led by the Spirit. I kindly explained to him that sometimes there are choices that seem right to us, but from God's perspective they are not.

He agreed, but stated that even if he had made the wrong choice, he was going through with it anyway. When I asked why, he readily replied that Jesus died on the cross to guarantee him the right to make wrong choices, to disobey, and to sin. He rationalized further that God's great love is so unconditional that no matter what wrong choices he may make, and no matter what he may do against God's will, that it should in no way affect their relationship. In his mind obedience or disobedience was just fine with God. Eventually he felt God would work things out for the best. My student chose to continue his promiscuous life, for he reasoned that God would love him and support his behavior anyway. After all, the blood of Christ assured him his freedom of choice.

Responsible Love

Apparently, the focus of my dear student was freedom but not obedience, presumption of acceptance in sin but not salvation from it. His hope was for me to join him in accepting and enabling him in the wrong decision he had already made. Accepting him and his choice was much more important to him than the choice itself. This is precisely what pervades the culture of tolerance today: intolerance of sin is considered a greater sin than sin itself. Of course, Jesus loves us and respects our freedom of choice; but much more importantly, He longs to save us from our wilfulness. His shed blood cries out to us from the cross to make the right choice, for it greatly grieves His heart when we abuse our freedom to make the wrong choice. Although He always respects our freedom, He pleads with us to cooperate with Him in deciding for righteousness and redemption. His heart was broken on the cross because of all the wrong choices made from Adam until now, why then carelessly break it again and again?

Paul knows that we are free to break the heart of Jesus afresh, and dishonor Him in our hearts and before the world. But why would we choose to treat the Jesus we love and obey this way! (See Heb. 6:6). Jesus sent the Holy Spirit, His representative, to convict us of "sin, and of righteousness, and of judgment" (Jn. 16:8). This holy conviction clearly shows the intention of the Spirit to lead us away from sinful choices unto righteous choices. There is no other way to face the judgment, without being covered with Christ's righteousness, and without intentionally choosing to follow Him and live His life.

The function of the Holy Spirit is to activate and implement what Christ desires in our soul. He exposes our ingratitude to Christ, reveals our callousness to our Savior's shed blood and tears, subdues our independent ways, and plants in our hearts divine enmity against sin. "The Spirit reveals the ingratitude of the heart that has slighted and grieved the Saviour, and brings us in contrition to the foot of the cross. By every sin Jesus is wounded afresh; and we look upon Him whom we have pierced, we mourn for the sins that have brought anguish upon Him. Such mourning will lead to the renunciation of sin" (*The Desire of Ages*, p. 300).

Liberty Not License

I know of a school principal who let one of his students use the school car. He let him drive it as long as he was careful. Yet he disregarded his caution, chose to drive recklessly, and he badly damaged it. The disappointed principal graciously took care of the damage, but admonished his careless student to heed his counsel next time. Imagine the principal telling him not to worry about the accident, but to instead focus on his free choice to drive carefully or recklessly–without admonishing him to choose to be careful. It would be hard to imagine such an improbable scenario.

The apostle Paul affirms the fact that we indeed have liberty in Jesus, but he cautions us that liberty is not license. "For you, brethren, have been called to liberty; only do not use liberty as an opportunity for the flesh, but through love serve one another" (Gal. 5:13). Use your liberty in choosing to honor and obey God, but not to gratify one's selfish desires. Even though

Christ's Way to Restoration

God never intended liberty to be license, a person can choose to make it so. Such misuse of liberty under the guise of free choice displeases God, and should never be encouraged in the slightest way.

Jesus took a big risk in giving His creatures the freedom of choice, because that is inherent in His eternal love. Adam made the wrong choice, thus plunging this world into the darkness of rebellion. We would not imagine that Jesus would have stood by passively, rejoicing that Adam had exercised his free choice to rebel. He was so grieved by such a wrong choice that He was compelled to rescue fallen humanity through His death. He ardently desired Adam to choose right, yet without any coercion. This wrong choice resulted in disobedience, sin, and death, for "the wages of sin is death" (Rom. 6:23). Undeservedly, Jesus took upon Himself humanity's sin and death as a direct consequence of the wrong choice. (See 2 Cor. 5:21).

Contemplate the horrendous cost that resulted from this original wrong choice: human misery and Christ's death. It makes every bit of sense that while Jesus respects our freedom of choice, He exhorts us to choose right, never saying either way works out for the good. The reason Jesus died was not to grant us free choice–for we already had it from the beginning–but it was to save us from the consequence of our wrong choice. If there was no wrong choice to begin with, Jesus would never have needed to die. It behooves us, then, to cooperate with Him in encouraging others in the valley of decision to make the right choices leading to restoration

Our freedom of choice is a wonderful gift from God. We need to join forces with Him to discourage people from making bad choices and to encourage them to make good ones. Tell me, aren't there already plenty of bad choices being made every day?

Free Choice But Right Choice

Don't we see their devastating consequences all around us? How can we then stand by passively and see people wreck their lives by their bad choices, while hiding behind free choice! Why not emphasize the freedom to choose right? Why not lovingly and intentionally encourage them to make the right choices in their lives? Is it not better to make it easier for them to choose right, and more difficult to choose wrong?

Choice Abuse

The first and foremost abuser of free choice was Lucifer. He was the most perfect and pure being God had created. His brightest and most brilliant angel, the covering cherubim of His dazzling glory. The Creator trusted him, who was perfect in all his ways, to be the closest to Him. God said this of him: "You were the seal of perfection, full of wisdom and perfect in beauty." And "You were perfect in your ways from the day you were created" (Ezek. 28:12, 15).

The Creator trusted him with the freedom of choice borne out of His loving heart. He had no reason to distrust Lucifer to make the right choices in loving submission to His benevolent will. It must have broken the heart of God to witness the abuse of freedom and the inception of rebellion in him. Such rebellion camouflaged in secrecy and deception, found fertile soil in a heart motivated by jealousy and pride. God's eternal plan for Lucifer was to remain a perfect being, but his wrong choice led him to become Satan.

For the first time the perfect God, surrounded by His perfect creation, witnessed first hand the outset of this deadly rebellion born out of a wrong choice. It must have been quite something to behold God tirelessly trying to persuade Lucifer to reconsider his wrong choice, in order to spare the universe of this catastrophic rebellion. In the book, *The Great Contro-*

versy, pages 495 and 496, we find these inspired insights about the anatomy of Lucifer's rebellion and God's awesome love and forbearance:

1. God exhibited great love and patience in laboring long with Lucifer. In the meantime, he was not cast away, showing clearly that God was deeply committed to win back his heart.

2. In spite of Lucifer's discontentment and move toward open rebellion, God repeatedly offered to forgive him, if he would simply repent from his unreasonable quest to have his own way.

3. Lucifer's gradual discontentment was indeed unreasonable, for he himself did not comprehend why he felt the way he did, and realized that such a feeling had no basis. What is so startling about this, is that Lucifer knew that his choice was wrong and God's plan was right, yet he persisted. He even knew that he would have been reinstated to his position on condition of humility and repentance.

4. But the costly pride of his self-centered opinion led him to deliberate and open rebellion. His gradual work done in mysterious secrecy and deception reached a point of no return, now bent on flagrantly usurping God's position and overthrowing His government.

5. Lucifer's rebellion had to do with the misuse of his God-given freedom of choice, and his view of God's law of love. The problem with Lucifer was that he simply *abused* the gift of his free choice. Plainly put: God desires and encourages His creatures to choose to obey Him out of love and appreciation of His ways. He encourages the use of such freedom to choose right, because therein lies universal peace and harmony. And although He grants them free choice, He discourages them from deciding wrong. "There was no note of discord to mar the celestial har-

monies. But a *change* came over this happy state. There was one [Lucifer] who *perverted the freedom* that God had granted to His creatures" (*Patriarchs and Prophets*, p. 35; italics supplied).

6. God labored long not to give Lucifer up to his wrong and determined choice. It broke His heart to see His perfect and trusted creature hold on to his rebellion. But when he persisted in his acknowledged waywardness, only then at this point of no return did God leave him alone. In His eternal wisdom God allowed Lucifer's rebellion to ripen fully into its ultimate outcome. God's creation needed to see the true character of God, and the resulting consequences of rebellion.

Pride and Jealousy

Lucifer was the epitome of perfection in wisdom, beauty, and in all his ways from the day he was created. It was indeed so "till iniquity was found in" him (Ezek. 28:15). As we live the horrible consequences of Lucifer's rebellion, two questions beg to be asked. First, what kind of "iniquity" was found in Lucifer's heart? The second question is more challenging. How could such "iniquity" sprout in the pure soil of so perfect a being? The answer to these questions have to do with Lucifer abusing his freedom of choice regardless of dire consequences. The Scriptures tell us the type of evil Lucifer harbored in his heart. Pride: "His [Lucifer's] heart was lifted up" (Ezek. 28:17). Jealousy: "I [Lucifer] will be like the Most High" (Isa. 14:14).

Ellen White gives us insights that shed light on the envy Lucifer felt toward Christ. What specific attributes was he envious of? Christ's *glory* and *power*. "And coveting the glory with which the infinite Father had invested His Son, this prince of angels aspired to power that was the prerogative of Christ alone" (*Patriarchs and prophets*, p. 35). Christ's *supremacy*. In his jealousy of Christ he determined to "dispute the supremacy of the Son

Christ's Way to Restoration

of God" (*Ibid.*, p. 36). He was also envious of Christ's *authority* and craved *equality* with Him. " These [rebellious angels] stood ready to second Lucifer's demand for equal authority with the Son of God" (*Ibid.*, p. 38). Christ's *honor*. Lucifer coveted the "honor which the infinite Father had bestowed upon His Son" (*The Great Controversy*, p. 494). Finally, he chose to allow "his jealousy of Christ to prevail, and he became the more determined" (*Ibid.* p. 495).

Lucifer's rebellion was gradual, and it took long for it to ripen into the open. God was far from being arbitrary in dealing with him, for He graciously granted him several lines of defense for recovery and restoration. Lucifer knew he was still greatly loved, and that forgiveness and reinstatement was his for the taking if he humbled himself. Tragically, he was severely conflicted in his heart, knowing well what was right but deciding against it.

This severe conflict in Lucifer's soul seemed to briefly abate when again he joined the angels in praising God. "Lucifer bowed with them, but in his heart there was a strange, fierce conflict." This conflict resulted from this: "truth, justice, and loyalty were struggling against envy and jealousy." It is strange that making the right choice to repent was so close to making the wrong choice to rebel. So close but so far away. "The influence of the holy angels seemed for a time to carry him with them. As songs of praise ascended in melodious strains . . . the spirit of evil seemed vanquished; unutterable love thrilled his entire being; his soul went out, in harmony with the sinless worshipers, in love to the Father and the Son." But alas, he was again "filled with pride in his own glory. His desire for supremacy returned, and envy of Christ was once more indulged" (*Patriarchs and Prophets*, pp. 36, 37).

Free Choice But Right Choice

By choosing pride over humility and insubordination instead of submission, he became more resistant to God's loving appeals. And his unyielding stubbornness led him to an unflinching determination to go his independent way no matter what. As if Lucifer's response to His Creator's loving, reasonable, and persuasive entreaties was like the saying: "I've already made up my mind, don't confuse me with the facts." He reached the point of no return, and burned every bridge leading to genuine repentance and restoration. Convinced that he was totally in the wrong, Lucifer clung ever tightly to his rebellion. And God had no choice but to cast him and his angels away from His presence.

Conflicted Mind

In the book, *The Story of Redemption*, pages 25-27, we find some unusual insights into Satan's conflicted mind. Cognizant of the stark reality of his rebellion, he became convinced that in his overreach he had lost everything and had gained nothing. Heaven's peace and joy were forever gone from him.

1. Satan regretted his enormous loss, wishing he could be reinstated to the peaceful atmosphere of heaven, but it was too late. This sentiment was not born out of genuine repentance, but out of disappointment and regret. "Could he [Satan] be again as he was pure, true, and loyal, gladly would he yield up the claims of his authority. But he was lost! Beyond redemption, for his presumptuous rebellion" (p. 25). Satan's concern had to do with the liability of his loss, not the loss of his love to God and His law.

2. The fallen angels, realizing their tremendous loss, were driven to an agitated state of blame and recrimination leveled at Satan and each other. As the saying goes, "Misery loves company," and now they were all miserable together.

Christ's Way to Restoration

3. Contemplating his awful fate, Satan trembled for fear of his ultimate demise. In desperation he desired an audience with Christ, hoping to negotiate a compromise out of his predicament. "His mighty frame shook as with a tempest. An angel from heaven was passing. He called him and entreated an interview with Christ. This was granted him. He then related to the Son of God that he repented of his rebellion and wished again the favor of God . . . Christ wept at Satan's woe but told him, as the mind of God, that he could never be received into heaven. Heaven must not be placed in jeopardy . . . The seeds of rebellion were still within him" (p. 26).

4. Spurned and separated with no hope, Satan desperately resolved to retaliate against God with everything at his disposal. His resigned attitude toward God was: either accept me or I will attack you, reinstate me or I will retaliate. "When Satan became fully convinced that there was no possibility of his being reinstated in the favor of God, he manifested his malice with increased hatred and fiery vehemence" (p. 27).

5. God knew that Satan's pent-up frustration would be unleashed in retaliation against Him and His holy beings, yet He stood firm for His eternal principles. He could not compromise with Satan's willful disobedience in the hope of appeasing him. Peace could not be secured at any price. "God knew that such determined rebellion would not remain inactive. Satan would invent means to annoy the heavenly angels and show contempt for His authority" (*Ibid.*).

6. Resentful and vengeful, Satan began his retaliation by harassing the holy angels, and seeking to separate Adam and Eve from God. "As he could not gain admission within the gates of heaven, he would wait just at the entrance, to taunt the angels and seek contention with them as they went in and out.

Free Choice But Right Choice

He would seek to destroy the happiness of Adam and Eve. He would endeavor to incite them to rebellion, knowing that this would cause grief in heaven" (*Ibid.*).

Lucifer and Judas

Consider for a moment the striking similarities between Lucifer's rebellion and Judas' deliberate betrayal of Jesus. They both wrongly thought that they were better at fulfilling God's divine plan by focusing on their own self-centered plans. Jesus' great act of condescension in washing Judas' feet stirred his hardened heart with love and the desire to repent. But again his pride exacted a costly price. "Jesus hungered for his soul . . . His heart was crying, How can I give thee up? The constraining power of that love was felt by Judas . . . When the Saviour's hands were bathing those soiled feet, and wiping them with the towel, the heart of Judas thrilled through and through with the impulse then and there to confess his sin. But he would not humble himself. He hardened his heart against repentance; and the old impulses, for the moment put aside, again controlled him" (*The Desire of Ages*, p. 645).

God did every thing possible to save Lucifer and Judas from themselves, but to no avail. In His agonizing love for them and heroic struggle to save them, He finally and reluctantly left them to their own deadly choice. The Bible is replete with such tragic consequences for choosing one's way instead of God's way. Lucifer's abuse of his free choice finds resonance also in the experiences of our first parents, their son Cain, king Saul, just to name a few. It all boils down to this: do I trust God, or do I trust self? Do I trust His choice for me, or rather my choice for myself? Do I trust His objective word to guide me, or do I choose to trust my subjective convictions? This does not mean that if we make missteps in choosing wrong He abandons us to our folly, but we should not continue to persist treading on Satan's enchanted ground. No one can be sure what the ultimate consequences of wrong choices can lead to, and the ripple effect it has on so many.

Christ's Condescension

We have already discussed the type of iniquity that Lucifer chose to indulge in: pride in his status and jealousy of Jesus. Now, let us attempt to deal with the other question: how could Lucifer a creature become jealous of Christ the Creator? In attempting to answer this question, let us begin by considering Christ's earthly condescension, and then proceed to consider His heavenly condescension. Look at the great contrast between Lucifer's disposition and that of Christ's. Lucifer, in his pride and envy craved to usurp Christ's position; Christ, in His humility emptied and lowered Himself to be a servant. Though both were at liberty to make free choices, Christ chose humility and salvation resulted, Lucifer chose pride and damnation resulted.

It is evident from Scripture that the virtue of divine condescension is an integral part of Christ's character. Such condescension was exemplified in His life, even from the foundation of the world, when He volunteered to redeem humanity. The apostle Paul depicts the condescension of Christ as self-emptying. The divine Son of God "made Himself of no reputation, taking the form of a bondservant" (Phil. 2:7). The literal translation of the phrase "no reputation" is to be rendered "emptying." The extent of this self-emptying was not only from the beginning, but the quality of it was to the extreme extent.

The beloved Son being equal with His glorious Father descended to the level of the worst criminal. This self-emptying revealed itself in Him taking the form of a submissive slave. The

Free Choice But Right Choice

Greek word for "slave" is *doulos*, referring to Christ's unquestionable submission all the way to the cross. This extraordinary kind of submission propelled Him to die the worst death–to descend from the uttermost glory to the uttermost debasement. Yet in surrendering His right to be equal with God, He was highly exalted above all. In total contrast to this, Lucifer craved a higher status than he was given, thus falling to total debasement.

This spirit of condescension is to be our experience as well. That is why Paul makes this personal application when He admonishes us to emulate Jesus' example of humility. "Let this mind be in you which was also in Christ Jesus" (Phil. 2:5). His whole life of condescension culminated in His sacrificial death on the cross. To have the mind of Christ is to have our hearts be broken with His heart for a lost humanity. The psalmist says: "The Lord is near to those who have a broken heart, and saves such as have a contrite spirit" (Ps. 34:18). Jesus was sent to "heal the brokenhearted" (Isa. 61:1).

But to have the humble mind and broken heart of Jesus is to fall on Him the Rock and be broken with contrition and humility. Jesus said, "Whoever falls on this stone will be broken, but on whomever it falls, it will grind him to powder" (Matt. 21:44). We must deal with the Rock. We must make use of our freedom of choice by heeding Christ's invitation to fall on Him. The only other free choice is to remain hard-hearted and wait for the Rock to fall on us in judgment. Why not now use our freedom of choice wisely, and fall on Him and be broken in contrition before it is too late. When Christians have been broken on the Rock, they come across like Jesus "gentle and lowly in heart" (Matt.11:29). They become patient, gentle, and grateful people. But those who have not yet been broken seem self-assured and overconfident. And there is an air of pride and arrogance about them.

Jesus being "gentle and lowly in heart" is a reflection of our heavenly Father's character.

That is what He told Philip: "He who has seen Me has seen the Father" (Jn. 14:9). Jesus came to planet earth to save lost humanity, and in the process reveal in all that He did what His Father was like. But He took the risk of being misunderstood and unappreciated in veiling divinity in humanity. That was God's best chosen way of self-revelation: becoming a man and being given a human name, Jesus. By appearing in this human form, the Jewish leaders misunderstood Him and esteemed Him not. They were baffled and enraged that, being a mere human, He claimed that He was the divine Son of God.

Jealous of Jesus

How could Jesus be divine, the Jewish leaders reasoned. He is just another human rabbi (misguided at that) like the rest of us. They were ready to stone Him for blasphemy, telling Him: "You, being a Man, make Yourself God" (Jn. 10:31, 33). His people were not only baffled at His wisdom and power, but jealous and offended. After all, how could He be so incredibly popular, so exceptionally mighty in words and works, being just one of them. Didn't they know His father, mother, brothers and sisters? He was just on their level; certainly to them He was no God. "So they were offended at Him. But Jesus said to them, 'A prophet is not without honor except in His own country, among his own relatives, and in his own house'" (Mk. 6:3, 4).

Normally jealousy is manifested among peers. It is reasonable to think that a student can be envious of another student's higher grades, or a laborer be jealous of his fellow laborer's success. But why would a student or a common laborer be envious of the position of president of the United States? It is a totally and vastly different realm. The Jewish leaders were resentful and envious of Jesus because they thought He was merely a man, on their level. Revealing God in human form was risky, opening the possibility for some to misunderstand Him.

Could it be that a similar thing happened in heaven? Could it be that God's Son revealed God to the angels in angelic form, just as He revealed God to humanity in human form? Here He was given a human name, Jesus; there He was given an angelic name, Michael. Could it be that He veiled His divinity in angelic form to convey what God was like to the angels? Could it be that Lucifer gradually became familiar with Michael, unawed by a fellow Angel? He possibly began to see Him as a peer with His humility and condescension, thus opening the possibility of envy. After all, he was not specifically jealous of the Father or the Holy Spirit, but only of Christ. Lucifer who "next to Christ, had been most honored of God and who stood highest in power and glory among the inhabitants of heaven" (*The Great Controversy*, p. 493).

How else could a creature be jealous of the Creator? If it is unreasonable for a common laborer to be jealous of the high position of the US president, why would it be reasonable for Lucifer, a mere creature, to be jealous of His Creator. Unless, of course, like the Jews he came to view Him as on an equal par with him. With this kind of gradual understanding and familiarity Lucifer experienced in relation to Christ, it would be understandable why he would be envious for not being included with Christ in the councils of God. Overcome with resentment for being excluded, he became envious of Michael, Whom he gradually thought as his equal. He learned that: "In all the counsels of God, Christ was a participant, while Lucifer was not permitted thus to enter into the divine purposes" (*Ibid*. P. 495).

Does God Ever Repent?

At this juncture this question is likely to cross one's mind: does God ever blame Himself for creating Lucifer who evolved into Satan? Remember that God created a perfect Lucifer, but Lucifer made himself into Satan by his own wrong choices. There was no devil out there to tempt him in his perfect environment, but by his pride and envy he created a devil within and out of himself. The blame falls squarely on Lucifer's wrong decisions. Consequently our first parents made the wrong choice, and their descendants who choose disobedience over obedience.

We may wonder if God regretted creating Lucifer in the first place. Does our changeless God ever change His mind when He surveys how things turn out to be? In Genesis 6:6 we learn that "the Lord was sorry that He had made man on the earth, and He was grieved in His heart." If God felt this way about creating man, He certainly felt this way about creating Lucifer. In some versions the verb "repented" is used instead of "was sorry." To experience repentance sounds so human, certainly not divine. Does God really repent like people do? For the righteous God to repent must be quite different than for sinful man to repent. "God's repentance is not like man's repentance . . . Man's repentance implies a change of mind. God's repentance implies a change of circumstances and relations. Man may change his relation to God by complying with the conditions upon which he may be brought into the divine favor, or he may, by his own action, place himself outside the favoring condition" (*Patriarchs and Prophets*, p. 630).

Some may argue that Lucifer's wrong choice was necessary to serve a greater universal purpose. Choosing wrong is always wrong and is never an inevitable necessity. "Man was created a free moral agent. Like the inhabitants of all other worlds, he must be subjected to the test of obedience; but he is *never* brought into such a position that yielding to evil becomes *a matter of necessity*. No temptation or trial is permitted to come to him which he is unable to resist. God made such *ample provision* that man need *never* have been defeated in the conflict with Satan" (*Ibid.*, pp. 331, 332; italics supplied).

Entitlement and Responsibility

A young man, confronted with a big decision to make, came to my office for advice. He became totally convinced that the crucial decision he was about to make was definitely wrong, yet he kept insisting that he had to go that way in order to get it "out of his system." I assured him that God still loved him even if he decided wrong and rebelled against God's word, but I strongly urged him, however, to choose trust and obedience to God. I emphasized that God ardently desires this, and has made ample provision for him to choose right. But unfortunately in this case, the more I encouraged him to choose God's way the more determined he became to choose his way. All along insisting that God loved him so much that He would sympathize with him and support his wrong choice. It is so true that "In all ages there have been those who claimed a right to the favor of God even while they were disregarding some of His commands" (*Ibid.*, p. 73).

Many godly parents I know are puzzled why some of their children choose to obey God and the others choose not to. They inherited the same genetic propensities of their parents, exposed to the same environment, experienced the same upbringing, and raised by the same values. Were they defective in rearing their rebellious children, but not in rearing the others? Should such parents ever blame themselves and be constantly consumed with regret? The fact is that sometimes, regardless of the home environment, some children's choices may be surprising. Sometimes under the best circumstances some siblings choose wrongly, and under the worst circumstances some choose rightly.

It is difficult to condemn or compliment, blame or bless, in these contradictory outcomes. The prevailing tendency in our culture is to often blame authority figures and providers. We blame parents, teachers, pastors, shopkeepers, and even God Himself. "The customer is always right" is the prevailing attitude. But realistically this is fallacious. The customer is not always right; and if we believe otherwise, we become enabling agents for unfairness and irresponsibility. It all has to do with people's choices–good or bad–and their consequences. Look at the household of the world's first dad and mom, and their two sons, Cain and Abel. Eve even entertained the high hopes that the older one would be the promised savior. Two brothers in the same home environment, but two radically different choices. Cain went about choosing wilful disobedience to God and rejecting his family values, and Abel choosing to do the exact opposite.

Where, then, does such puzzling outcome of affairs rest? How does God see this from His perspective? You see, God loved both brothers equally, but viewed their behaviors differently: He approved of the younger's conduct but disapproved of the conduct of the older, all based on their different choices. "Cain had the same opportunity of learning and accepting truths as had Abel. He was not the victim of an arbitrary purpose. One brother was not elected to be accepted of God, and the other to be rejected. Abel chose faith and obedience; Cain, unbelief and rebellion. *Here the whole matter rested.*" (*Patriarchs and Prophets*, p. 72; italics supplied).

Free Choice But Right Choice

Love and Truth

We clearly witness this pattern of outcome in families throughout human history. For "Cain and Abel represent two classes that will exist in the world till the close of time" This then should not unduly surprise or baffle us when it occurs in our earthly household, for it indeed happened in God's heavenly household. How should we then relate to all of this? We need to take utmost care in how we reach out to the ones who choose to follow the example of Cain. We need to speak the truth in love to them. We need to be loving but not compromising, gracious but not approving, kind but not enabling of their wrong choices. We need to lovingly and prayerfully plead with them to turn away from their wrong choices and move toward the right choices.

The apostle Paul counsels us to speak "the truth in love" (Eph. 4:15). *The Desire of Ages* echoes this Pauline approach in dealing with others: "Christ Himself did not suppress one word of truth, but He spoke it always in love . . . He fearlessly denounced hypocrisy, unbelief, and iniquity, but tears were in His voice as He uttered His scathing rebukes" (p. 353). Here is where we have to watch out for extremes. Some speak the truth without the love, others love without the truth. Both extremes are deficient and damaging. To speak the blunt truth without love is harsh and legalistic, and to love without daring to speak the truth is mere shallow sentimentalism that calls for no accountability.

Why not faithfully follow the balanced, loving, and truthful approach of Christ in dealing with the failings of others, regardless of consequences? Thus we give others the greatest incentive to return to God. We will not succeed with all to be sure, but we may at least help to save some. We must never be discouraged, when our earnest entreaties are ignored; in fact, they may very well resent us and become more determined to live out their wrong choices. Thus in the process of their rebellion, they spread their influence far and wide. For example, the devastating effects of Cain's choice to defy God's will influenced generations to come, leading eventually to total destruction by the Flood. "The forbearance of God only rendered the wicked more bold and defiant in their iniquity" (*Patriarchs and Prophets*, p.78). But no matter how negative the response of others may be, we must represent Christ in lovingly beseeching them to submit to God. At least they know there is a true representative of Christ among them.

Moral Backbone

That is why we must be very careful and wise when counseling others about the choices they make. While respecting their freedom, we are not to leave them with any ambiguity about the need to choose right. We are to clearly impress upon their minds the superiority of deciding in favor of God's word. We must not leave in our approach any room for doubt, neutrality, or presumption in this crucial matter. Paul had no qualms about this certainty whatsoever. His readers knew where he stood in his exhortation to them. Notice the strong words he uses –"plead," and "implore"–in his urgent appeal to make the right decision: "Now then, we are ambassadors for Christ," he writes, "as though God were pleading through us: we implore you on Christ's behalf, be reconciled to God" (2 Cor. 5:20).

To many modern psychologists and counselors the biblical injunctions seem too intrusive. Often, after listening for hours to people's problems, they deliberately take a passive attitude. It is up to you, they counsel, whatever you decide is okay as long as you decide. But either way is not okay. Coercion must never be used, and people's choices must always be respected, but neither should we counsel them in the "whatever" mode. Why should we stress this persuasive approach to choose right? Because major life decisions are in the process of being made, and human destinies hang in the balances–genuine love calls for nothing less.

The godly parents of Samson did not think that going along their son's wishes was the right choice for them or for him. Being pleased by something should never be the crucial criteria for our sympathy and support. Samson was quite pleased with a certain Philistine woman, and he pressured his parents to acquiesce: "Get her for me," he demanded, "for she pleases me well" (Judg. 14:3). We learn from this story that Samson's parents tried to encourage him to make the right choice and discourage him from making the wrong choice. They even offered him ideas of how to go about marriage the right way. Even though their wise counsel was not heeded, yet they go on record as courageously standing up for the right choice albeit the risk of alienating their only beloved son.

Lessons from Aaron

Look at what happened when Aaron was so passive in dealing with God's wayward people wanting to worship a golden calf. His irresolute approach in this case was certainly different than his courageous brother Moses. Keep in mind that Aaron was the spiritual leader of Israel and Moses' right-hand man. Yet when it came to this crisis of decision he was found fearful and faint-hearted before the people. He was entrusted with God's people to encourage good in them and to restrain evil, yet he showed no moral backbone to stem the tide of rebellion. Indeed it was he himself who "received the gold . . . fashioned it with engraving tools, and made a molded calf" (Ex. 32:4). And this was not all: in his passive cowardice he even drifted into open idolatry by building an altar for the idol and proclaiming a feast for the Lord (v. 5). Strangely enough, he tried to camouflage this naked idolatry in a cloak of religiosity, mixing idol worship with God's worship. Imagine the low moral levels spiritual leaders fall into when they passively and cowardly go along with people's whims.

With a heightened sense of righteous indignation, Moses rebuked his brother, placing responsibility squarely upon his shoulders. "What did this people do to you," Moses asked, "that you brought so great a sin upon them?" (v. 21). Moses knew the answer to his question for he "saw that the people were unrestrained (for Aaron had not restrained them, to their shame among their enemies), then Moses stood in the entrance of the camp, and said, 'Whoever is on the Lord's side, let him come to me'" (vs. 25, 26). In response, Aaron gave such a lame excuse for not restraining the people, seeking sympathy from his brother: "You know the people, that they are set on evil" (v. 22).

It is so tragic that there are modern-day Aarons who bend to whatever pleases those in their charge. Those entrusted with positions of spiritual leadership, and those significant others, can positively influence the vulnerable ones bent on taking the wrong course. If they support and enable such to follow what pleases them, the Lord will not hold them guiltless. The only safe way in these situations is to bravely advocate the honor of God and His commandments. Remember what the wise man said: "There is a way that seems right to a man, but its end is the way of death" (Prov. 14:12). Modern-day Aarons should stand strong in the integrity of the Lord they represent, to encourage others to choose the right and shun the wrong. "Some men have no firmness of character. They are like a ball of putty and can be pressed into any conceivable shape . . . There is an

Free Choice But Right Choice

indomitableness about the Christian character which cannot be molded or subdued by adverse circumstances. Men must have moral backbone, an integrity which cannot be flattered, bribed, or terrified" (*Testimonies*, vol. 2, p. 297).

We must learn valuable lessons from the experience of old Aaron. It is put there for our admonition, we who are living in these last days before Christ comes. Many a crisis of decision for right or wrong will confront us as we prepare for the time of trouble. Such crises demand a "man of firmness, decision, and unflinching courage; one who held the honor of God above popular favor, personal safety, or life itself" (*Patriarchs and Prophets*, p. 316). Here are some of the tragic consequences incurred and decisive opportunities missed when Aaron went along with what pleased the crowd instead of what pleased God:

First of all, Aaron's vacillation rendered the people more determined to follow their own inclinations. Second, his cowardice in yielding to the rebellious desires of the people encouraged them to sin. Third, his insult to God by camouflaging manifest rebellion in a cloak of religion. Fourth, his ambivalent posture in compromising truth with error, the right choice with the wrong choice. Fifth, his desire to please the people bent on rebellion blinded him to the enormity of the crime against Jehovah he was allowing to be committed on his watch. Thus thousands were needlessly and tragically lost. Sixth, his cowardice to stand for truth aggravated the dire situation. "If Aaron had the courage to stand for the right, irrespective of consequences, he could have prevented that apostasy" (*Ibid*., p. 323). Seventh, his tacit tolerance of others to sin was hideous before God. "Of all the sins that God will punish, none are more grievous in His sight than those that encourage others to do evil" (*Ibid*., pp. 316, 317, 323).

Christ's Way to Restoration

God is convicting our hearts to make a right choice. There are too many Aarons, and too few Moseses. Therefore, are we going to be like pliant Aaron or like resilient Moses? "And there are still pliant Aarons, who, while holding positions of authority in the church, will yield to the desires of the unconsecrated, and thus encourage them in sin" (*Ibid.* p. 317). Sacred history shows that Aaron was a great leader for God, who stood faithfully by his brother Moses. They proved to be a formidable duo for righteousness, fighting unitedly the Lord's battles. Yet in this catastrophic event of sanctioning Israel's wanton idolatry, his record was marred. The Lord was about to destroy him along with the rebels, but spared him for his earnest repentance and the intercession of Moses.

Let us dare to be a Moses, standing for the truth no matter what the cost. Let us learn from pliant Aaron the devastating cost of compromise. Let us not just emphasize our freedom of choice, but also of making the right choice. This precious gift of free choice was never meant to be abused but intended to be used to trust and obey God's word.

Discussion Questions

1. How do you love others without enabling them in their wrong choices and conduct?

2. Paul writes about Christian liberty. How can we enjoy such liberty without license?

3. Should we be neutral or intentional in facilitating people's choices? Why or why not?

4. Was Lucifer's jealousy of Christ's position "reasonable" in any way? Compare this with the Jewish leaders' jealousy of Him.

Free Choice But Right Choice

5. Love without truth, and truth without love. Discuss these two extreme approaches in helping others. Where do you find the balance?

6. What helpful lessons may we learn from Aaron's vacillation? How can we have a moral backbone in a permissive society without hindering our witness?

7. Discuss the dynamics of a conflicted mind. How does God's word help resolve this?

CHAPTER TWO

Divine Enmity

"I hate cancer, I just hate it! It took away the only son I have!" Cried out an anguished father who just lost his teen-age son to the ravages of cancer. Cancer is one of many dreadful things that is a result of sin. And if we hate the devastating plague of cancer, how much more we should have hatred toward the malignant cancer of sin. It is obvious that none of us in our right mind want to hold on to cancer, to the contrary we strive valiantly to get rid of it. Yet it is so strange that many of us cuddle the cancer of sin in our heart without feeling the desperate need to avoid it at any cost. If we do not allow the Great Physician to help us get rid of it, then inevitably it will get rid of us. If we continue to cherish darling sins in our lives and embrace them instead of Jesus, then we will be destroyed along with them.

Sin Is Serious

God takes sin seriously and hates it passionately. The Son of God in counsel with His Father volunteered to sacrifice His life for man if he ever chose rebellion. Yet when our first parents succumbed to sin, the Father found it quite difficult to let go of His only Son to carry on His mission of destiny. It was heart-wrenching for Him to imagine His pure and perfect Son suffer and die a horrible death under the crushing load of human sin and depravity. "Long continued was that mysterious communing" between the Father and the Son for fallen humanity. "The plan of salvation had been laid before the creation of the earth . . . yet it was a struggle for the King of the universe to yield up His Son to die for the guilty race" (*Patriarchs and Prophets*, p. 63).

Sadly, our fallen first parents did not take their transgression seriously. They presumed, like many do today, that if their Creator so loved them that He would overlook their rebellion, or at least minimize its dreadful consequences. They became cognizant of what they had done, but "both flattered themselves that He who had given them so many evidences of His love would pardon this one transgression or that they would not be subjected to so dire a punishment as they had feared" (*Ibid.*, p. 57). Only when they learned from Christ and the angels that their wrong choice to rebel would cost the Son of God His life, they began to realize the enormity of what they had done.

Our decision to distrust God and disobey His law may not seem serious to us, but to Him it is very serious. His eternal law is the reflection of His character and the foundation of His government. In spite of His eternal love for Adam and Eve, He could not put His law aside. If He did, the universe would have plunged into the abyss of chaos and destruction. As we say in our democratic society, no one is above the law. If this is true with human law, certainly it must be even more so with His divine law. No one in His vast universe is above the law, not the holy angels and not even Christ Himself. "The claim that Christ by His death abolished His Father's law is without foundation. Had it been possible for the law to be changed or set aside, then Christ need not have died to save man from the penalty of sin" (*The Great Controversy*, 466).

Christ's Way to Restoration

Divine Resolution

Our heavenly Father always has us and all creation on His mind and in His heart. Consequently, He devised a plan to maintain the integrity of His law, the harmony of the universe, and the salvation of doomed humanity. In order to find the balanced and perfect resolution to this crisis, Christ stepped up to take our place and suffer the consequences of our wrong choices. This divine resolution resulted from Christ's initiative in becoming our Substitute, in dealing with our sin and consequent death.

The apostle Paul aptly captures this resolution in Romans 6:23. "For the wages of sin is death, but the gift of God is eternal life in Christ Jesus our Lord." Also God "made Him who knew no sin to be sin for us, that we might become the righteousness of God in Him" (2 Cor. 5:21). What an awesome exchange! Exchange our sin for His righteousness, and our death for His life. The "wages" of sin exchanged for the "gift" of Christ's eternal life! With the requirements of God's eternal law came His plan of redemption. If the demands of the law could even be slightly deviated from, then Christ would never have needed to die such a cruel death. In Christ's atoning sacrifice "Mercy and truth have met together; righteousness and peace have kissed each other" (Ps. 85:10). His vicarious death is solid evidence that sin could not by any means be ignored. If God takes sin so seriously, so should we. One look at the Son of God hanging on the cross should cause us to never regard sin frivolously or inconsequentially.

The only way our first parents would be spared death, was for them to trust in the promise that someday Christ would sacrifice Himself for their disobedience. The first hint of that hopeful promise is found in Genesis 3:15 when Christ addressed the woman along with the serpent. " I will put enmity between you and the woman, and between your seed and her Seed; He shall bruise your head, and you shall bruise His heel."

There is hope kindled by the promise. Christ and His faithful ones will suffer through the ages, but ultimately He will conquer Satan. There is a great contest here between the bruised head and bruised heel, between the Seed and the Serpent. But praise God, the bruised heel of the Seed will ultimately crush the head of the Serpent. This was the divine verdict that was delivered in the Garden. "All of this is foreshadowed in the first prophecy: 'I will put enmity . . . ' And this will continue to the close of time" (*The Great Controversy*, p. 507).

Does God Ever Hate?

God created this "enmity" in the human heart against evil that was not there. Then He planted the hope that someday the Redeemer would destroy Satan and restore Eden. There is a correlation between the creation of enmity and the planting of hope. You see, Satan thought that he had it made. He planned on no enmity but cooperation between him and humanity. He counted on man being so depraved that he would be henceforth controlled by him and remain loyal to him. With no enmity towards him, he was sure he would have full sway in the affairs of fallen humanity. Remember, this "enmity" is not at all of human origin, but it is of divine origin. It was God's creative act of putting it where it did not exist before, hence it is *divine* enmity.

Satan hoped he would have peace and harmony with fallen humanity, thus joining him in opposing God. But when Satan learned that God would plant enmity against evil in the human heart, "he knew that his efforts to deprave human nature would be interrupted; that by some means man was to be enabled to resist his power" (*Ibid.*, p. 506). Fortunately, God is always a step ahead of Satan—undermining his schemes, and undergirding our desire to shun evil. Thus through His grace, we are empowered to break free from this demonic stranglehold. In the confusion of human surmising, why not place our trust in God who is ready to shatter the enemy's grip on us, so that we may be set free to hate what He hates and love what He loves.

It might seem strange that we are discussing the subject of divine enmity alongside divine love. What is the connection between love and hatred? How could a God who planted love in the heart also plant hatred? What kind of "enmity" did He create? We need to remember that God did not create evil but enmity for evil. It is revealing that the psalmist establishes a direct link between loving God and hating evil. In fact, hating evil is an expression of loving God, and results in our safeguard against it. "You who love the Lord, hate evil! He preserves the souls of His saints" (Ps. 97:10). What brought about such enmity? And how can it be an expression of God's love, His grace, and protection?

Satan's Subtle Schemes

In the previous chapter, we considered the inception of envy and pride in Lucifer's heart. Here we will consider his subtle ways of deception. Multiple of shrewd schemes camouflaged in a veneer of altruism for the well-being of God's creation. Disguised as such, while taking full advantage of his respected and trusted position as the nearest creature to God, it was Lucifer's "policy to perplex with subtle arguments concerning the purposes of God. Everything that was simple he shrouded in mystery, and by artful perversion cast, doubt upon the plainest statements of Jehovah. And his high position, so closely connected with the divine government, gave greater force to his representations" (*Patriarchs and Prophets*, p. 41). He availed himself of unfair advantages by employing beguilement, duplicity, and fraudulence.

He used deceptive schemes to the hilt for he well knew that God, crowned with righteousness and girded with truth, could never use such tactics. God well knew what was in the treasonous and treacherous mind of Lucifer to accomplish his plans. "God could employ only such means as were consistent with truth and righteousness. Satan could use what God could not—flattery and deceit" (*Ibid.*, p. 42).

Let us look more closely at Lucifer's subtle and deceptive means to reach his goal. In him was exhibited the perfect manifestation of the saying: "The end justifies the means." Also "Win at any cost."

1. Lucifer used deception cloaked in altruism. He was the flawless embodiment of what Jesus said: "Beware of false prophets, who come to you in sheep's clothing, but inwardly they are ravenous wolves" (Matt. 7:15). The most pernicious thing in destroying relationships can be found in those closest to us. Those totally trusted in one's family, one's church, or homeland can under certain circumstances become the most formidable opponents. Civil servants, thoroughly acquainted with their nations's intelligence, may cause untold harm if they become traitors. Trusted and charismatic church leaders can bring about disgrace and shame if they choose to betray their faith.

Cherished and trusted family members, who are well acquainted with the inner sanctum of their families, may become bitter enemies if they defect. They are thoroughly acquainted with their families' strengths and weaknesses, securities and vulnerabilities, and they are steeped in their family values. Thus, they have the potential of becoming the most loyal allies or the bitterest enemies. Consider here the extremities Jesus predicted would occur even with the closest of relationships: "Now brother will deliver up brother to death, and a father his child; and children will rise up against parents and cause them to be put to death . . . And a man's enemies will be those of his own household" (Matt. 10:21, 36).

2. Lucifer cleverly employed subtlety and perplexity in building up his case against God's pure intentions for His created beings. He absolutely had no case except the one his envious heart conjured up. In our judicial system today, a case with absolutely no evidence would be readily thrown out of court. But using subtleties to complicate matters, he hoped to diffuse doubt and distrust where there was none.

3. He used cunning perversion to take what was simple and recast it in mysterious complexity. Therefore, to invent a problem where none had existed, he abused his persuasive skills, intended for good, to buttress his supposed evil. A bad teacher is one who takes something simple and makes it complicated; on the other hand, a good teacher takes something complicated and makes it simple. In this sense, Lucifer proved to be a very bad teacher: he took something plain and made it very complex. We too are sometimes guilty of taking the plain directives of God and spin them according to our own desires.

4. Lucifer took unfair advantage of his trusted and elevated position nearest to his Creator to disseminate false insinuations on unsuspecting angels. And his status conveniently strengthened such covert schemes. The angels under his care gave him the benefit of the doubt, thinking that such a trustworthy leader would not intimate such doubts without a cause. That is why we must always be careful to weigh what others say by the standard of God's word, especially those in trusted positions. It is curious, isn't it, that the name "Lucifer" means light, yet he chose

to love darkness more than light. You see, God intended that he would live out the message of his name to shine brightly with the light of His truth. Now he was conflicted, casting his lot on the side of his own dark deceptions.

Those who choose darkness are fearful that their deeds may be revealed, but those who choose light are willing for their deeds to be seen. Jesus was right when He said this about the darkness of deception: "For everyone practicing evil hates the light and does not come to the light, lest his deeds should be exposed." And this is what He said about the light of truth: "But he who does the truth comes to the light, that his deeds may be clearly seen, that they have been done in God" (Jn. 3:20, 21). Therefore, let us always be secure in the light of God's unchangeable truth, for the prince of darkness is intensifying his subtle deceptions just before Christ's return. This is God's standard for security: "To the law and to the testimony! If they do not speak according to this word, it is because there is no light in them" (Isa. 8:20).

5. Lucifer carried out his deception as if the rules of engagement in this conflict–fair play, justice, honesty, and truthfulness–did not apply to him but only to God. He would employ anything at his disposal to win, for to him the end justified the means. If you were in God's place, how would you deal with this dilemma? How would you figure out what to do when you have a friend who pretends to tell you the truth, only to deceive you? Who pretends to be reliable, only to prove unreliable? Someone who looks you straight in the eye and lies with a straight face? Someone who changes the agreed-upon rules in the middle of the game? The only answer to this untenable situation is to pray, seeking God's wisdom. To stay above the fray, to say what you mean and mean what you say, let the situation run its course, and trust God to accomplish His will.

Christ's Way to Restoration

It is true that God loves the sinner but hates the sin. After all, sin brought havoc and devastation to His harmonious universe. He must hate sin because Lucifer's rebellion wiped out a third of His angelic host, caused the fall of our first parents, plunged their human family into misery, and brought about the dreadful death of His only Son. We must be grateful to God for creating this enmity towards evil in our hearts, for without it we would not genuinely return to God. "It is the grace that Christ implants in the soul which creates in man enmity against Satan. Without this converting grace and renewing power, man would continue (to be) the captive of Satan, a servant ever ready to do his bidding" (*The Great Controversy*, p. 506).

What would we do to repulse Satan's attacks without the impulse of this divine enmity? Such an impulse gives us the power to overcome our bent to evil. Ellen White asserts that this divine impulse accomplishes the following: First, it creates conflict within us; second, it enables us to resist evil; third, it leads us to abhor sin; and fourth, it proves that God is leading us. "But the new principle in the soul creates conflict where hitherto had been peace. The power which Christ imparts enables man to resist the tyrant and usurper. Whoever is seen to abhor sin instead of loving it, whoever resists and conquers those passions that have held sway within, displays the operation of a principle wholly from above" (*Ibid.*).

Resolute Resistance

What difference does this make in our daily Christian walk? If in fact sin is so dreadful and deadly, and Satan is fighting with all his cunning to make it seem irresistible, then why aren't we uniting ourselves with Christ in resisting him? Knowing that our eternal destiny is on the line, why don't we then seek God with all our hearts. This ever-present problem is caused by laziness in following Christ and laxness toward sin. God's word is replete with exhortations to flee iniquity, to resist evil, and to die to sin. For example: "Therefore submit to God. Resist the devil and he will flee from you" (James 4:7). Also "Resist him [the devil], steadfast in the faith" (1 Pet. 5:9). The context of such biblical exhortations is intentionality, gravity, and urgency. Not a hint of frivolity or laxity here.

Why do we become so careless about evil, thus experiencing no enmity against it? Like a skilled general, the evil one maliciously plots to defeat us. Why then don't we place our whole trust in our mighty God to defeat him? Tragically, we often flee before him instead of him fleeing before us. "Why is it that he meets with no greater resistance?" Ellen White asks. "Why are the soldiers of Christ so sleepy and indifferent?" (*The Great Controversy*, p. 507). Then on the same page she diagnoses this vexing problem, giving reasons for its presence:

1. These "soldiers of Christ" hardly experience a vital relationship with Him. They are not walking closely with Him in their daily lives.

2. They do not experience the generating power of the Holy Spirit to empower them to hate and resist evil.

3. From their perspective, they do not view sin as something hateful. They fail to view it as exceedingly malignant and deadly.

4. They do not walk away from it, for to them it is not something to exercise themselves over. Therefore, they do not diligently seek God's help to resist it with all their power united with His formidable power.

5. Thus, there is "little enmity against Satan and his works, because there is so great ignorance concerning his power and

malice, and the vast extent of his power against Christ and His church. Multitudes are deluded here" (*Ibid.*).

Let us honestly face this fact: If Lucifer succeeded in deceiving the pure angels in a perfect heaven, why wouldn't he succeed in deceiving fallen human beings in a wicked world? Therefore, there must be no doubt about taking him seriously. That is why the apostle Peter warns us to "Be sober, be vigilant." Why should we? "Because your adversary the devil walks about like a roaring lion, seeking whom he may devour" (1 Pet. 5:8). As "soldiers of Christ," how can we then be "so sleepy and indifferent"? Why not now choose to have a vital relationship with the Captain of our salvation, and be awake and resolute to fight the fight of faith?

There is certainly a good reason, on our part, for a holy vigilance against evil. Satan has been sharpening his skills of deception since his original rebellion. We are definitely no match for him without total submission to Christ, for he has been in this deceptive business for such a long time. He tries to manipulate us on many fronts: psychological, spiritual, rational, and social, to name a few. No wonder it is so indispensable to have solid enmity for him and determined vigilance against him.

Contemplate these sobering insights about the psychological games Satan plays with our minds, especially in these last days: "For thousands of years Satan has been experimenting upon the properties of the human mind, and he has learned to know it well. By his subtle workings in these last days, he is linking the human mind with his own, imbuing it with his thoughts; and he is doing his work in so deceptive a manner that those who accept his guidance know not that they are being led by him at his will. The great deceiver hopes to so confuse

Divine Enmity

the minds of men and women, that none but his voice will be heard" (*Selected Messages*, bk. 1, pp. 352, 353).

Lack of enmity against evil leads us into the slippery path of beguilement and delusion. It is this enmity that helps us to be wary and watchful. Can you imagine such a level of deception! He imparts the unwary with his thoughts, controls their minds, and leads them in his ways so subtly that they imagine it to be their own thoughts and ways. Sometimes it does not even stop there, but it descends to such delusional and dangerous levels, attributing those deceptions to God Himself.

Dangerous Delusions

I once counseled a supposedly devout pastor who ascribed his deluded convictions to God's leading in his life, even though such convictions went squarely against God's plain word. I remember him responding defensively to my entreaties to follow God's word: "But I know that God impressed me with this; I feel very strongly about it."

Consequently, he brought ruin into his life, insisting all along he was doing God's will not Satan's. Such deluded personal convictions, falsely attributed to God, were put above biblical imperatives. He argued circuitously that even if he were deluded by Satan's thoughts, he would still be alright, for God would eventually work things out for the good. So to him, either way was a win-win situation; yet he overlooked one important detail: the *condition* to God's promise that "all things work together for good." God's promises are always conditional, and the condition here applies to "those who love God, to those who are called according to His purpose" (Rom. 8:28).

The deceiver is multiplying his efforts in these last days because he knows he has but a short time. Only those who hate

41

evil and love truth will be safe in this world which is held hostage to his delusions. This is specially applicable in our modern age of electronic wizardry. Our only security is in Jesus and His word as we face Satan's decisive and final battle for the manipulation and control of the human mind. He already has much control through entertainment, hedonism, tolerance of sin, and depravity. Things are presented in such a subtle way that what is evil seems truth, and vice versa.

In such a polluted environment, we cannot always trust even our own senses. God's wants our senses to be imbued with His mind, for we "have the mind of Christ" (1 Cor. 2:16). It is like being on a roller coaster, or on a plane tossed all around by a raging storm. This storm is so blinding that we cannot depend on our subjective feelings to tell us our position, altitude, or direction. And we must realize that the only safe way is to look at the objective truth shown on the instrument panel. In a world gripped by Satan's storm of vicious delusions, our only course is to trust our skilled Pilot Jesus, and His instrument panel the Bible.

In these final hours of earth's history, every one of us will be tested to the core. Will our present faith prove to be anchored in Christ? "By the sifting of temptation the genuine Christian will be revealed. Are the people of God now so firmly established upon His word that they would *not yield to the evidence of their senses?* Would they, in such a crisis, cling to the Bible and the Bible only? Satan will, if possible, prevent them from obtaining a preparation to stand in that day" (*The Great Controversy*, p. 625; italics supplied).

It is quite sobering to contemplate that Lucifer's clever tactics succeeded in deceiving a third of the holy angels. Therefore, if such tactics succeeded so well in perfection there, why would they not succeed in imperfection here? Only one third made the choice to follow him, the other two thirds chose to follow Christ. Satan could not override their free choice by coercing them to choose his way. "Satan's work began in heaven by suggesting doubts, questions and thoughts in such a subtle way that unfallen angels were not aware that they were being led by him. They uttered thoughts that *originated with him*, thinking they were *their own*" (*Patriarchs and Prophets*, pp. 35-40; italics supplied).

Boasted Independence

The human mind, what an intricate invention! If enlightened by the Spirit it is so capable of good, but if deceived by Satan it is so capable of evil. If it is beguiled by the enemy it can play perverse tricks on the mind. If his insinuations are dwelt on, and if his ideas are repeated, they can become entrenched in the psyche and believed as truth. People deluded into such falsehoods gradually become so blinded that it is almost impossible to dislodge them from their hardened positions. They spiritualize away God's evidence, and rationalize their rebellion; so much so that they come to think that they are obeying Him. Sin no longer appears sinful to them, and instead of hating it they defend and cherish it.

Add to all of this mix the extreme individualism and reckless independence of our western culture, which insists on having our own way regardless, defending it as a sacred right. People are encouraged and enabled to do their own thing regardless of consequences, and they come to expect supportive treatment of their rebelliousness. Such reckless independence is treated almost like a god to be worshipped. Yet the religion of Christ calls on us to give up our ways and to submit to His ways. "Boasting of their independence they will, under his specious, bewitching influence, *obey the worst impulses of the human heart and yet believe that God is leading them.* Could their eyes be opened to distinguish their captain, they would see that they are not serving God, but the enemy of all righteousness. They would see that their *boasted independence* is one of the *heaviest fetters* Satan can rivet on unbalanced minds" (*Testimonies*, vol. 5, p. 294; italics supplied).

The only answer to this dilemma is to love Jesus and to cling to His righteousness, and in His name to hate and resist evil. Let us be clothed in Christ's mighty armor. "Finally, my brethren, be strong in the Lord and in the power of His might," Paul urges us. "Put on the whole armor of God that you may be able to stand against the wiles of the devil. For we do not wrestle against flesh and blood, but against principalities, against powers, against the rulers of the darkness of this age, against spiritual hosts of wickedness in the heavenly places. Therefore take up the whole armor of God, that you may be able to withstand in the evil day, and having done all, to stand" (Eph. 6:10-13).

Discussion Questions

1. "There is a way that seems right to a man, but its end is the way of death." (Prov. 14:12). What are some wrong ways that seem right to us? How do we discern such ways and avoid them?

Divine Enmity

2. How do we reconcile the fact that God loves yet He hates? What does God hate, and why?

3. Lucifer succeeded in deceiving perfect angels in heaven. To a much greater extent he can succeed in deceiving imperfect human beings like us. What safeguards has God provided to help us defeat him in our daily lives?

4. "Are the people of God now so firmly established upon His word that they would not yield to the evidence of their senses?" (*The Great Controversy*, p. 625). How do we answer such a question? What is the relationship between God's objective truth and our subjective experience?

5. What does the phrase "boasted independence" mean as discussed in this chapter?

CHAPTER THREE

Salvation from Sin

One semester I was teaching a course in eschatology, and in one lecture I was explaining how Jesus came to save us from the deadly cancer of sin. In the middle of my lecture, I was rudely interrupted by a student habitually tardy to class. Catching the idea that I was saying bad things about sin, he blurted out: "You are wrong, professor, sin is fun!" Caught off guard, I wondered how to respond. "You are right," surprising him and the class. "Satan makes sure that sin is fun. But let me contrast the kind of fun Satan offers with the kind of fun Christ offers."

The students were now paying close attention, so I proceeded to elucidate further about the kind of fun Satan offers with sin: It leaves a bad taste in the mouth afterwards, and on the next day a spiritual "hangover." Then its fun does not last long, but it is temporary. And when we come to the end, Satan comes by to exact his wages, which is death, and the second death at that. "For the wages of sin is death" (Rom. 6:23). However, the type of fun Jesus gives us is of a quality that leaves a wonderful taste in the mouth. It continues in the form of the abundant life here. Then at the end, Christ comes along not to deprive us of life but to grant us eternal life. We must see the vast contrast between the first part of Romans 6:23 and its second part.

Salvation from Sin

Contrast between the wages Satan exacts and the gift that Christ offers. "But the gift of God is eternal life in Christ Jesus our Lord."

The Spirit of God convicted my heart to earnestly appeal to my students to use their gift of choice to side with the winner Jesus and choose to reject the loser Satan. Thank God, two dozen of my students stood up for Jesus, including the one who earlier interrupted my lecture. It is amazing how the Holy Spirit marvelously worked to defeat Satan's designs. That student had no idea that his disturbance of the class led to his own conversion and the conversion of several of his classmates.

Life in the Blood

It is revealing that in our society the focus in life is on having fun. Friends greet you, "are you having fun?" Others report that they are having great fun. Everybody, it seems, is trying to have fun in life, as if fun should be life's first priority. Why not first ask, what is the *right* thing to do instead of what is the *fun* thing to do? When we endeavor to do the right thing in honoring God, He consequently provides us with genuine fun.

Why choose to cozy up to sin instead of crucifying it? Why cuddle sin in our bosom without fearing its scorching fire? Why would anyone in their right mind hold on to malignancy rejecting a permanent cure? The most hateful thing to our loving Father is sin, because it killed His only Son and brought misery and devastation to His creation. That was the primary reason why God sent His beloved Son to this world: to rid us of sin for good. You see, often in the Scriptures a person's name represents character, or signifies a message or a mission. The Son of God was given a special name when He was incarnated to signify His mission to planet earth. The angel Gabriel revealed to Joseph Heaven's choice for this special name: "And she shall bring forth a Son, and you shall call His name Jesus, for He will save His people from their sins" (Matt. 1:21). John echoed this thought when he wrote that Christ "was manifested to take away our sins, and in Him there is no sin" (1 Jn. 3:5).

The name "Jesus" in Hebrew is *Yeshua*, meaning "Yahweh is salvation." Salvation is found in the person of God Himself, not in an ideology. In other words, when you submit yourself wholly to God you receive salvation. But whenever salvation is necessary, then logically it is salvation from something detrimental. *Webster's Dictionary* defines "salvation" as "being saved from danger, evil, difficulty, destruction." After Gabriel revealed this special name, he gave the reason why: "He shall save His people from their sins." How was this salvation from sin to be accomplished? Through Jesus becoming sin for us who knew no sin (2 Cor. 5:21). Notice the essential logic of His salvation of people *from* their sins, not *in* their sins. How can an oncologist save his cancer victim *in* cancer! To the contrary, he expends all his acquired skills to save him *from* cancer.

Did Jesus have to die to save us from sin? Some give different reasons, as if such reasons were something optional to be dispensed with. They say that the principal reason He died was to show us God's love, or to show us a good example to follow. I am all for God's love and for a good example, but the real reason was to save us from our sins. Sin is the big culprit here, because it demands the wages of death. Sin has to be gotten rid of in order for death to be defeated. If we imagine otherwise, how would we explain away the priority of the sacrificial system practiced among God's people since Abel's sacrifice? Long before righteous Abel, the Son of God was "the Lamb slain from the foundation of the world" (Rev. 13:8).

Salvation from Sin

What was God's plan from the foundation of the world to deal with sin? The giving of life through the shedding of blood. "For the life of the flesh is in the blood, and I have given it to you upon the altar to make atonement for you souls; for it is the blood that makes atonement for the soul" (Lev. 17:11). The only One who could give life by the shedding of His blood is the One who is the Source of life. No angel or other created beings could ever do that, for they borrow life from Christ the Source. From the Garden of Eden to Calvary, God provided such a vivid and painful object lesson of the enormous cost of sin. A mighty message of salvation that was written in blood from the first lambs slaughtered to clothe Adam and Eve, to the Lamb of God slain at Calvary to redeem us.

In Leviticus 17:11, the word "atonement" for the soul is used; and in Hebrews 9:22 the word "remission" of sin is utilized. The first term refers to a *covering* of blood for the sinful soul, the second word refers to *forgiveness* from sin through the blood. Both terms have to do with dealing with the sin problem, covering or forgiving it, through Christ's shed blood. All the lambs slain in Israel pointed to the promised Lamb of God who would come someday to cover sin, to forgive sin, and to remove sin through His supreme sacrifice. John the Baptist had the awesome privilege of announcing the fulfillment of the promise of Christ's sacrifice. When John saw Jesus coming to him for baptism, he fervently exclaimed: "Behold! The Lamb of God who takes away the sin of the world!" (Jn. 1:29).

The verb rendered to "take away" is from the Greek verb *airo*, which literally means to "lift up," to "bear away," or to "remove." John testifies in Revelation 1:5 about Jesus' blood that washes us from sin. "To Him who loved us and washed us from our sins in His own blood." What is abundantly clear from all these renderings is that Christ's precious blood is shed to *get rid of sin*. The words of this hymn ring so true: "There is a fountain filled with blood, drawn from Immanuel's veins; and sinners plunged beneath that flood, lose all their guilty stains."

The slain Lamb of God is to vicariously liberate us from the bondage of sin. "But He was wounded for our transgressions, He was bruised for our iniquities," and He "shall justify many, for He shall bear their iniquities" (Isa. 53:5, 11). Here is the "bruising" of the Seed's heel (Gen. 3:15) fulfilled in connection with the divine enmity God created against evil. Christ's choice to shed His blood was clearly to rid of sin for all time. He was driven by a such costly mission: He spilled His blood to save us from our sins. Shortly before He was to be crucified, He said to His disciples: "For this is My blood of the new covenant, which is shed for many for the remission of sins" (Matt.26: 28).

Make It Easy to Sin?

There is not the slightest hint in all the Scriptures that God considers sin lightly. How can we look at the dreadful situation of our world, and the devastation sin has brought about with indifference! Yet, in spite of all this mayhem still too many are nonchalant about sin. A teenager came by my office for counseling about her parents' attitude regarding a certain sinful behavior. They reasoned with her that because Jesus loved her unconditionally, He would understand and sympathize with her promiscuous tendencies. They told her that the biblical injunctions about moral purity are nice but too idealistic in our modern daily life. I will never forget her disappointment in her parents' reckless counsel: "I am trying to be a good girl, but I wish my parents would not make it so easy for me to sin."

Is it our goal to presume on God's love by making it easy for people to disobey? Isn't God's love meant to impact our lives in leading us to trust and obey Him? If that isn't the thrust of the biblical message, then Christ's mission to save us from our sins would have been in vain. Our sacred calling is to encourage struggling people, while using every possible incentive, to please and obey God. The pendulum has swung too far, I think, in the direction of cheap love with license to sin, not responsible love with empowerment to live for Christ.

Empowering Grace

Also the pendulum has precipitously swung too far in the direction of cheap grace. But what would we do without God's grace? We are indeed saved by it. "For by grace you have been saved through faith" (Eph. 2:8). But what kind of grace are we talking about? The cheap and irresponsible kind, or the costly and responsible type? Yes, grace is God's unmerited favor, but such favor must not be misused to excuse misbehavior. God has built into His costly grace the power to overcome evil. This grace does not only provide enmity against evil, but resistance and power over it, so that Satan's grip might be broken. It also leads to genuine conversion, to radical change from cherishing what is evil to loving what is good.

Consider the following facets of God's costly yet undeserved favor. Notice that this grace converts and enables the soul to live righteously. "It is the *grace* that Christ implants in the soul which creates in men *enmity* against Satan. Without this *converting grace* and *renewing power*, man would continue the captive of Satan, a servant ever ready to do his bidding. But this *new principle* in the soul creates *conflict* where hitherto had been peace. The *power* which Christ imparts *enables* man to *resist* the tyrant and usurper" (*The Great Controversy*, p. 506; italics supplied).

It helps to keep in mind what the apostle Paul said about grace and the potential for it to be taken for granted. If some misused even Paul's correct and balanced teaching on grace, then why would they not misuse this gift today? The danger always exists in the unrenewed heart of relating to such an important gift in an unbalanced way. Paul responds emphatically to such: "Shall we continue in sin that grace may abound? Certainly not! How shall we who died to sin live any longer in it? (Rom. 6:1, 2). The apostle James joins Paul in affirming this balanced approach to grace. He links the giving of God's grace to the humble in heart who choose to submit to Him in resisting the devil. "But He gives more grace. Therefore He says: 'God resists the proud, but gives grace to the humble.' Therefore submit to God. Resist the devil and he will flee from you" (James 4:6, 7).

Driving on the freeway recently, I found myself absentmindedly cruising at 85 mph. I was hoping at that moment that a highway patrolman would not be in the vicinity, but to my dismay, there he was waiting for me. Like a flash of lightening he took off after me, and I knew for sure I was in trouble. Bringing my car to a stop, I started praying and urging my wife to pray too. From my rearview mirror I could see him holding his ticket pad, ready to give me a well-deserved citation. Suddenly, to my total amazement, he looked at me and said, "Sir, it's your lucky day, just got an emergency call, and I've got to go."

I felt quite relieved, grateful, and amazed for the grace God and the highway patrolman had shown toward me. Pausing to thank God, I proceeded to drive while carefully watching the speed limit this time. Grace motivated me to carefully keep the law out of sheer gratitude. Imagine if I had misused this grace by speeding again, with the lame excuse that grace was shown toward me earlier that day; and that if I were stopped repeatedly for speeding, I would expect no speeding tickets, but grace only. That would surely be inexcusably presumptuous. God intends His grace to lead us to genuine repentance, to inspire grateful obedience, and to empower us to follow Jesus wherever He leads. It makes total sense, doesn't it? If this costly grace led Christ to the cross, it should certainly lead us to love and obey Him with all our heart.

Trendy Tolerance

Oftentimes we hear this expression: "God loves the sinner but hates the sin." This is a balanced approach, as it should be, in relating to sinners and their sinful behavior. Some lean toward the attitude of hating sin and sinners too. In recent times, the pendulum has swung too far in the direction of emphasizing loving sinners and accepting their sin as well. All done under the prevailing popular god of tolerance. So here is the progression in that ever-swinging pendulum: from hate sinner hate sin, to love sinner hate sin, and to love sinner love sin. Now in this post-modern age, willful sinners are so emboldened, they want others to not only love them but to also sympathize with and approve of their sinful behavior. This comes under the subtle guise of benign terms such as "acceptance," "support," "tolerance," and "approval."

Such want to have it both ways: they want the love of Jesus but also the love of the world. They desire God's approval while insisting on doing their own will. They deliberately choose to be prodigal sons and daughters, rationalizing that God loves them no matter what, and thinking that someday they will eventually return to Him. They confuse unconditional love with unconditional acceptance and approval, saying that if others don't approve and support their misguided behavior they are not being loved. Moreover, they become even more emboldened to the extent that they are discontent with unconditional love and misguided approval, endeavoring to change and control such into their own image.

Christ's Way to Restoration

Of course, there is nothing new under the sun, even the issue at hand. This self-centered strategy was conceived in the heart of Lucifer. Not only did he desire unconditional love, sympathy, and approval from the Creator and his fellow angels, but he was bold and brazen enough to actually endeavor to change the changeless God, to alter His immutable law, and to overthrow His righteous government. *The Great Controversy*, pages 495-500, offers great insights in discerning Lucifer's subtle strategy. He intimated that God's laws "imposed *unnecessary restraint*" on His creatures. All his mental powers were "bent to the work of deception, to secure the *sympathy* of the angels." He concealed his deceptive work under a "specious *profession of loyalty* to God. He claimed to be seeking to promote the *honor of God*, the *stability of His government*, and the *good of all* the inhabitants of heaven" (italics supplied).

Although he was the source of discontent in heaven, he made it appear that such discontent was already in existence. "When he urged that *changes* be made in the *order and laws of God's government*, it was under the pretense that these were necessary in order to *preserve harmony in heaven*." He was so boldly ambitious that he planned, after securing the angels' sympathy and support, to change the rest of the perfect universe. "Satan thought that if he could carry the angels of heaven with him in rebellion, he could *carry the other worlds*" (italics supplied). The unquenchable ambition of Lucifer did not stop with the desire for some personal independence, but gradually escalated to an elaborate conspiracy to change God or otherwise overthrow Him. Satan's real intention was evident when he subjected Christ to the temptation of offering Him all the world if He would simply worship him. His ultimate ambition was nothing less than to overthrow God as the One to be worshiped (Lk. 4:5-8).

Salvation from Sin

But in spite of all his crushing defeats, Satan has never given up. He refuses to budge one iota in his ambition and determination to overthrow God Himself. In his overreach, he will carry this defiant attitude all the way to the final showdown by marshaling his forces and attacking the holy city. After the thousand years in heaven, the holy city will descend and Satan will be released for awhile. During this final time he "will go out to deceive the nations which are in the four corners of the earth, Gog and Magog, to gather them together to battle, whose number is as the sand of the sea. Then they went up on the breadth of the earth and surrounded the camp of the saints and the beloved city. And fire came down from God out of heaven and devoured them" (Rev. 20:8, 9).

Satan will imagine that the loving God will not have the heart to destroy so many billions of His creatures, and that God will possibly flinch in the stark face of such utter devastation. He will assume that God will go through a grieving phase over the loss of so many fallen angels and human beings, but that He will get over it. Maybe, just maybe, with enough show of force and fortitude, there will be a slim chance to bend God's will to his own will. And why not, after all, he will have nothing to lose. However, God will not flinch but will proceed with His strange act of destroying rebels and rebellion: fire comes down and consumes them all. Then and only then will Satan get the point about God and His reality.

Restless Rebels

How does his rebellion apply to our rebellion today? Are there some characteristics in Lucifer's rebellion similar to ours? What makes rebellion so dangerous is that we know we have chosen the wrong course but persist in it anyway. Becoming adamantly determined in our rebellion, we go out of our way to justify it. Our own conscience convicts us of our inner conflict, of an unsettling disequilibrium. So in order to cope, we are driven to find sympathy and support for our behavior. Fueled by our own pride and self-centeredness, we press headlong in our entrenched defiance.

Cooperation with Christ brings about equilibrium and peace in our lives, and we become settled on who we are and what we are about. Consequently, we do not have this driving force to get sympathy and support for our conflicted existence. The saying, "Misery loves company," is so true in this connection. Such misery leads to restlessness, which leads to searching for those who would agree with us and even follow our example. And we become so desperate for such acceptance, that we would even twist and manipulate any counsel to our own advantage.

"The apostate is *never at rest*, except as he obtains *sympathy* and *support* by *inducing* others to *follow his example*" (*The Great Controversy*, p. 505; italics supplied). Such rebellion is never self-contained, but spreads out in ever-widening circles. This defiant mind set does not merely call for loving sinners, but for accepting and enabling their sinning, and even becoming changed by it. And we are dismayed by such reckless brazenness until we learn about the dark powers behind it. "For this reason fallen angels and wicked men unite in desperate companionship" (*Ibid.*). This was precisely Lucifer's seductive and winning strategy with the angels, and ever since he has been practicing it so successfully on human subjects. That is why determined and stubborn people should not surprise us much, for they are in league with evil powers who egg them on in their willful rebellion.

Out of genuine concern, we try to reach such people with truth spoken in love. Disagree with their insubordination, as we must, but disagree agreeably. We must always remember that in life there is always hope for everyone to be saved, and with God's help we succeed in saving some. But it is extremely difficult to make any headway with some people who are determined to have their own way. Consequently, we are placed between a rock and a hard place, so to speak. If we kindly listen to them, they make themselves believe we agree with them or even desire to be like them; but when they discover that we do not, they feel a letdown. Thus they set themselves up for disappointment, and begin to lash out in criticism and accusation.

If we try to lovingly work with them, they could become defensive and resentful, ready for attack. Paul writes Timothy about the usefulness of this biblical counsel: "All Scripture is given by inspiration of God, and is profitable for doctrine, for reproof, for correction, for instruction in righteousness" (2 Tim. 3:16). But such counsel upsets them because it goes against the notion of wanting help, for they feel the need to be accepted and supported in their waywardness. That is why so many good people compromise their principles by showing unconditional acceptance and support, against their best judgment. They conclude that if they do not compromise they could face even more intransigence. And this plays right into the rebels' minds, for they know that they would often bend others to their way by their persistence.

Would our loving and judicious God have compromised with Lucifer and his rebellious host for the sake of getting along or to secure appeasement? Never, for peace could not be secured at any price. While showing His love, He also maintained His principles regardless of consequences, knowing full well that this could bring about separation and war in heaven. But taking such a wise stand was best for the whole universe in the long run. You see, compromise on the surface seems desirable and helpful, but the ill consequences can be boundless. What has been happening on planet earth, in this regard, is but a microcosm of what had already transpired in heaven. "The *same spirit* that prompted rebellion in heaven still inspires rebellion on earth. Satan has continued with men the *same policy* which he pursued with the angels" (*The Great Controversy*, p. 500; italics supplied).

Peace at Any Price?

In ages past during the period of apostasy and persecution of Christians, compromise and faithfulness were seen for what they were. The time of trouble is fast approaching, and our faith will be tested in the furnace of persecution. Will it be consumed as stubble or refined as gold? "To secure peace and unity they were ready to make any concession consistent with fidelity to God; but they felt that even peace would be too dearly purchased at the sacrifice of principle. If unity could be secured only by the compromise of truth and righteousness, then let there be difference, and even war. Well would it be for the church and the world if the principles that actuated those steadfast souls were revived in the hearts of God's professed people" (*The Story of Redemption*, p. 324).

It is likely that when you try to point the willfully disobedient back to God, they would resent it. This may happen in spite of your sincere expression of kindness, understanding, and patience. "Reproof of sin still arouses the spirit of hatred and resistance. When God's messages of warning are brought home to the conscience, Satan leads men to *justify* themselves and to seek the *sympathy of others in their course of sin*. Instead of correcting the errors, they excite *indignation* against the reprover, as if he were the sole cause of difficulty" (*The Great Controversy*, p.500, italics supplied). There is certainly a risk in caring enough to lovingly correct someone's disobedience. They may pour out their wrath on you, imagine fault in you, or project their own problems on you in order to justify themselves.

The tragedy is that they imagine and reiterate their misrepresentations and untruths so many times that they come to actually believe their self-deceptions to be truth. They feel they have to do this as a coping mechanism to relieve their conflicted selves. The rebellion of Korah and his friends is a case in point. They had gone too far until they convinced themselves that wrong was right, treason was loyalty, and sin was righteousness. "Like Korah and his companions, many, even of the professed followers of Christ, are thinking, planning, and working so eagerly for self-exaltation that in order to gain the sympathy and support of the people they are ready to pervert the truth, falsifying and misrepresenting the Lord's servants, and even charging them with the base and selfish motives that inspire their own hearts. By persistently reiterating falsehood, and that against all evidence they at last come to believe it to be truth. While endeavoring to destroy the confidence of the people in the men of God's appointment, they really believe that they are engaged in a good work, verily doing God service " (*Patriarchs and Prophets*, p. 404).

On a practical note, we need to be wise when we give audience to the opponents of truth. They come and subtly present their preconceived ideas and hidden agendas. We desire to show civility and respect to them, so we listen and show sympathy. But we do not want to react to their notions because we do not want to get involved in their rebellious schemes. Leaving our presence, we later learn they are taking our civility and attentiveness as support of their views. In their blind ambition they try to change us to join their cause, otherwise they turn against us.

Christ's Way to Restoration

Christ was absolutely faultless in heaven and on earth, yet Lucifer made unfounded accusations against Him, so did His Jewish opponents. Pilate, a heathen despot, declared His innocence three times (Jn. 18:38; 19:4, 6). The Roman governor was eager to placate the mad mob, and his conscience would have been relieved if he had found some basis for condemnation, but he could not. Certainly if he had found Christ guilty of sedition against Rome, he would have been obligated under Roman law to exact capital punishment. Christ testified that when Satan came to Him he found no fault in Him. Therefore Satan's accusations were totally fabricated. If Christ being so perfect was the subject of such misrepresentation, why would it surprise us to be treated similarly.

Remember how the Jewish leaders were so indignant when they heard Christ speak truth to them. Having already decided against Him, they urged others to do likewise. Can you imagine them accusing Jesus of being crazy and demon possessed! "And many of them said, 'He has a demon and is mad'" (Jn. 10:20). It is so preposterous that our Lord, most sober and sound, the demons' archenemy, was so unfairly vilified. As He proceeded to talk to them about being the good shepherd of the flock and His relationship to His Father, they became so livid that they "took up stones again to stone Him" (v. 31). This was the second time they had tried to kill Him, but they had one more go at Him. "Therefore they thought again to seize Him, but He escaped out of their hand" (v. 39). Toward the end of His mission, their murderous anger burst out on Him as He was led to the cross. As Simon was carrying His cross, He turned to those lamenting His suffering and uttered these sobering words: "For if they do these things in the green wood, what will be done in the dry?" (Lk. 23:31).

Salvation from Sin

Active and Passive Virtues

But what sort of approach should we use with the erring ones? For sure we want to be gentle, loving, and understanding; but that is an incomplete picture, for we also need to balance this with courage, earnestness, and firmness. Ellen White encourages us to have such balance in our way of helping others. She calls the former virtues the "passive" ones, and the latter virtues the "active" ones. The "Christian life is more than many take it to be. It does not consist wholly in gentleness, patience, meekness, and kindliness. These graces are essential; but there is a need also of courage, force, energy, and perseverance . . . Those who would win success must be courageous and hopeful. They should cultivate not only the *passive* but the *active* virtues. While they are to give the *soft answer* that turns away wrath, they must possess the courage of a hero to resist evil. With the charity that endures all things, they need the *force of character* that will make their influence a positive power" (*The Ministry of Healing*, pp. 497, 498; italics supplied).

So, what is Christ's way of dealing with lostness, waywardness, or rebellion? Christ Himself answers this question in presenting three consecutive parables recorded in Luke 15:1-24. First, the parable of the lost sheep; second, the parable of the lost coin; and third, the parable of the prodigal son. On careful examination of these parables, we notice that they show progressive intensity in the dynamics of lostness. Yet Christ demonstrates a specific and hopeful approach in dealing with the increasing complexity of each case.

The first parable depicts a person who loses his way and becomes stuck in the affairs of this world. Yet he wants out of this predicament. He admits he is lost, but does not know how to find his way out. He cannot help himself, so he calls out to the Good Shepherd to rescue him. And the response of the Shepherd is to leave everything behind and rush to his rescue, carrying him on his shoulders to the safety of the fold.

The second parable deals with the lost coin in the household, which represents a lost person who does not know he is lost. However, if told the truth about his situation he would want to be found. And the response of the woman, who represents Jesus, is to spare no effort in searching diligently, never stopping until she finds the lost coin.

The Path and Peril of the Prodigal

However, the problem of the prodigal son becomes much more intense and serious because:

1. He knows well that his father loves him greatly and wants the best for him in every way.

2. He knows that leaving his father and going to a far country to live a worldly life is not the right thing to do, neither for himself nor for his father.

3. He also knows that receiving his inheritance prematurely, that is to say while his father is alive, is an insult and shows a total lack of respect for his father.

4. He well knows that everything about his plan to depart from home is self-centered and rebellious, yet he chooses to deliberately compromise his conscience and leave anyway.

5. He can be sure that a loving father such as his gives his son every possible incentive to stay home, enjoying a loving and trusting relationship with him, but upon his son's insistence to leave anyway, the father cannot do anything more except to sadly let go. The son deliberately chooses to be a prodigal, not caring about the consequences to himself, his father, his family, and his community.

Salvation from Sin

6. It is interesting that the father does not rush after his son, pleading with him to return, but lets him go on his way. He does not follow him to his parties to show his sympathy and comradery, neither does he go to join him in feeding the pigs. If in fact he does that, he would come across to his son as compromising his principles, and hence enabling him in his rebellious course of action. The son's action is the cause for the disruption of the father-son relationship. The father remains the same as always, but the son chooses to go against his family values, replacing them with other values. Remember that it is the son himself who insists on leaving home.

This opposite outcome is made clear in the tragic experience of another father, Eli, who enabled his sons' rebellion by his indulgent love and tolerance of their evil actions. Ellen White describes Eli's misguided approach toward his sons as "mistaken kindness," which resulted in the "death to his wicked sons, and destruction to thousands in Israel" (*RH*, Aug. 30, 1881). This concept of "mistaken kindness" is very telling in this context. The clear implication here is that irresponsible behavior toward the rebellious is often camouflaged not only by mistaken kindness but by a mistaken concept of love, grace, and support. Such a mistaken approach hinders rather than helps the prodigal by exacerbating the problem and making it worse.

7. The father's love is the genuine and responsible kind, the love that is tough and holds the son accountable for his actions. Such a loving heart can only persuade not coerce, appeal to him to stay but not force him to stay. He cannot stop his beloved son from leaving, and cannot follow him in his folly. But his beloved son never ceases to be on his mind and in his heart. The wise and patient father knows that sometimes rebellion has to take its course before genuine repentance can occur. He also knows that only through this kind of responsible love can his son have

the greatest incentive and possibility to come back home in true repentance. Luke 15:20 clearly shows that the father is eagerly hoping for his son to repent and return: "And he arose and came to his father. But when he was still a great way off, his father saw him and had compassion, and ran and fell on his neck, and kissed him." The words of the hymn are so apt here: "Time after time He has waited before, and now He is waiting again to see if you are willing to open the door: O how He wants to come in."

8. Not all prodigal sons come to themselves in contriteness of heart and in genuine repentance. Some mistakenly think that all prodigals come back, but this is not true. Happily, however, the story of this one ends on a positive note. The prodigal's heart is softened, and in humility he "came to himself." Recalling to mind the abundant blessings he used to enjoy at home, he longs to go back at any cost. His is a genuine repentance evidenced by his contriteness and broken-heartedness.

This was the kind of attitude he had when he finally decided to come to himself. One can surmise that as this young man left home he also left himself, and became a different person. In his defiance, it seemed that he had put aside his real self for awhile and had taken on a new self. This untenable transition from one self to another was not sane, as if he had taken leave of his own senses. He was sort of brainwashed in the sense that he allowed outside forces to transform his beliefs and attitudes. But the hardship and famine humbled and compelled him to reconsider his ways, and come back to his senses. And of course the father, who always waited and prayed and hoped, welcomed him with open arms.

Sadly, however, some prodigals choose not to repent and return to their senses. If the prodigal son had decided to cling

Salvation from Sin

to the idols of his self-centeredness and rebelliousness, then he would not have returned. The father could have ever loved him, constantly prayed and hoped for him; but that would have been of no avail unless the son had responded. That is why we must be very careful in counseling others in making crucial decisions, especially the youth. The emphasis in our counsel ought never to be merely free choice but right choice. It should never be: you got to hurry and decide, a good or bad decision is not the point, just the freedom to decide. Some misguided counselors insist that whatever you decide, to be a prodigal or not to be is not the question, just decide. Either way is okay, and God eventually and somehow will work things out.

Saul the Prodigal

King Saul was a prodigal who never returned to God's favor. His was a classic case study of willful insubordination that never changed to genuine repentance and obedience. Carefully studying this anatomy of rebellion in 1 Samuel chapters 9-15, and chapters 60 and 61 of *Patriarchs and Prophets*, we glean the following helpful insights:

1. God wanted to give Saul, Israel's first king, every advantage to become a righteous and successful ruler. Physically endowed: a most handsome young man in all Israel, with an impressive physique. Spiritually gifted: anointed by the Spirit, chosen and consecrated for leadership, converted into a new man, and given a new heart.

2. God launched Saul's leadership with such great promise. He knew that he would have his share of mistakes, but given a new heart, He hoped Saul would have a humble and submissive spirit. Unfortunately, the opposite happened: he was not only foolish in disobeying God's command and usurping Samuel's role in offering a sacrifice, but presumptuous and full of blame

and excuses. "There is no safety except in strict obedience to the word of God. All His promises are made upon condition of faith and obedience" (*Patriarchs and Prophets*, p. 621).

3. All during his rule, Saul never learned true humility before God. He would often choose to compromise, then excuse and rationalize his disobedience. He was a prime example of practicing situation ethics. He would do wrong then compensate for that with religious acts, as if God could not see the intent of his heart. "Saul was in disfavor with God, and yet unwilling to humble his heart in penitence. What he lacked in real piety he would try to make up by his zeal in the forms of religion" (*Ibid*. p. 622).

4. God was very patient and longsuffering with Saul. Though he brought dishonor to God and his high calling, yet "his errors were not irretrievable, and the Lord would grant him another opportunity to learn the lesson of unquestioning faith in His word and obedience to His commands" (*Ibid*. p. 627). And soon enough Saul's final opportunity was near at hand when God commanded him to utterly destroy the Amalekites. Yet he again presumed on God's mercy and patience, and flagrantly disobeyed His explicit command. With no sense of guilt or remorse, he dug himself even deeper in his presumptuous and precipitous rebellion, flagrantly flaunting his disobedience.

5. Even though Samuel was Saul's wise mentor, held in great regard by him, he disregarded his counsel, and became offended and defensive at his reproof. He recklessly squandered the enormous blessings of having Samuel not only as his able mentor, but as his spiritual father who loved him as his own son. Lacking humility and gratitude, he felt ill at ease around Samuel, and thus minimized his contact with him. As if we could hear him think aloud to himself: "Either Samuel loves me, accepts

and approves what I do, or else I don't want to see him." In other words, approve of me or depart from me.

6. God's and Samuel's patience toward Saul was risky in the sense that he chose to become more emboldened in his rebellion. God's longsuffering toward the disobedient either softens or hardens their hearts. Yet He keeps trying again and again because He "has no pleasure in the death of the wicked, but that the wicked turn from his way and live" (Ezek. 33:11).

7. Samuel grieved bitterly over Saul's deliberate disobedience. He wept and prayed all night pleading with God to give his beloved Saul another chance. Early the next day he set out to meet Saul– now flush with victory and pride rekindled in his heart–hoping against hope that he would see his error and truly repent. "With an aching heart the prophet set forth the next morning to meet the erring king. Samuel cherished a hope that, upon reflection, Saul might become conscious of his sin, and by repentance and humiliation be again restored to the divine favor. But when the first step is taken in the path of transgression the way becomes easy. Saul, debased by his disobedience, came to meet Samuel with a lie on his lips" (*Ibid.*, p. 630). He was ready now to boldly defy the truth of God's word, preferring to obey his own selfish impulses than God's solemn commands.

8. The rebel is restless unless he finds those who would tolerate his prideful acts and lame excuses. The mark of his trade is disobedience camouflaged with partial obedience, obstinacy obscured by pretended pliancy, and self-justification heralded as reasonableness. All of this is done under the guise of religious acts. Saul desired to sacrifice the best of the sheep and oxen upon the altar of disobedience without first sacrificing his heart on the altar of obedience. In other words, while his mouth professed obedience, his heart possessed disobedience. That is why

Samuel responded: "Behold, to obey is better than sacrifice, and to heed than the fat of rams. For rebellion is as the sin of witchcraft, and stubbornness is as iniquity and idolatry." Then God's fearful and final verdict was pronounced against Saul: "Because you have rejected the word of the Lord, He also has rejected you from being king" (1 Sam. 15:22, 23).

9. Like Lucifer before him and Judas after him, Saul expressed sorrow for his willful disobedience too little too late. Terrified by this fearful sentence, he felt horrible sorrow for his catastrophic loss, not for his stubborn disobedience. "I have sinned," he began his contrived confession, "for I have transgressed the commandment of the Lord and your words, because I feared the people and obeyed their voice. " There he goes again with another excuse. All along he apparently was ready to obey his own voice and the voice of the people, but not God's voice. It seems he was determined to excuse his disobedience until the bitter end. Then he pleaded for pardon: "Now therefore, please pardon my sin, and return with me, that I may worship the Lord" (1 Sam. 15: 24, 25). Contrast this kind of contrived confession with David's contrite confession. David's confession was immediate, genuine, and complete. Upon hearing prophet Nathan's reproof, he simply confessed: "I have sinned against the Lord" (2 Sam. 12:13) without any fanfare of ifs and buts.

10. By repeatedly resisting the Spirit that anointed his rulership, Saul resisted the only means by which God could rescue him from his self-destructive behavior. It was "he who had willfully separated himself from God" (*Ibid.*, p. 634). Although Saul fought witchcraft within his nation and idolatry without, yet he strangely found both in his own heart. The hideous evils of witchcraft and idolatry were manifested in his stubbornness and rebellion. The clearest depravity was shown when Saul consulted the witch of Endor. His powerful bewitchment and "fa-

Salvation from Sin

tal presumption must be attributed to satanic sorcery. Saul had manifested such great zeal in suppressing idolatry and witchcraft; yet in his disobedience to the divine command he had been actuated by the same spirit of opposition to God, and had been as really inspired by Satan as are those who practice sorcery; and when reproved, he had added stubbornness to rebellion" (*Ibid.*, p. 635).

Persistent and Perilous Presumption

The following solemn warning should be heeded by each one of us, no matter how spiritual or religious we may think we are. Remember that Saul who was earlier controlled by the Spirit, was later controlled by Satan. "It is a perilous step to slight the reproofs and warnings of God's word or of His Spirit. Many, like Saul, yield to temptation until they become blind to the character of sin. They flatter themselves that they have had some good object in view, and have done no wrong in departing from the Lord's requirements. Thus they do despite to the Spirit of grace until its voice is no longer heard, and they are left to the delusions which they have chosen" (*Ibid*).

There is no doubt whatsoever that all have the freedom of choice, but we should encourage them to make right choices. Why take the risk of playing spiritual roulette with vulnerable people, risking that they may never come back? Why not emulate the example God has set before us? Although He does not force our will, yet He pleads with us to make the right choice, and entreats us to turn from our ways and follow His way. But if we ignore His pleadings and continue to persist in going our way, then He reluctantly allows us to live the consequences of our wrong choices. And if we continue to cling to the garments of sin and rebellion, then God will reluctantly have to deal with us as He deals with the garments we have become so attached to.

There is a popular but dangerous way of dealing with waywardness today: no loving exhortation or reproof, only tolerance and acceptance. Some well-meaning people show mistaken kindness by not showing enough love and courage to speak the truth. They tolerate what they should not for fear of alienating others, but in actuality they end up enabling them to continue in their rebellion. Of course, they may initially resist the light because they do not like their dark deeds to be corrected. "But the Lord reproves and corrects the people who profess to keep His law. He points out their sins and lays open their iniquity." And why does He do that? For many good reasons: "He wishes to separate all sin and wickedness from them, that they may perfect holiness in His fear and be prepared to die in the Lord or be translated to heaven. God rebukes, reproves, and corrects them, that they may be refined, sanctified, elevated, and finally exalted to His own throne" (*Testimonies*, vol. 2, p. 453).

Look at the loving and reasonable way God dealt with His wayward people as seen in the book of Hosea. He drew them unto Himself with gentle cords of love, He taught them how to walk, eased their heavy burdens, and even stooped down to nourish them (Hos. 11:1-4). But the more He treated them this way the more they pulled away from Him. "Ephraim has encircled Me with lies, and the house of Israel with deceit" (v. 12). "My people are bent on backsliding from Me," He laments. Yet in spite of all their rebellion, He pleads with them with a heavy and broken heart: "How can I give you up, Ephraim? How can I hand you over, Israel? . . . My heart churns within Me; My sympathy is stirred" (vs. 7, 8).

Salvation from Sin

But if God's people are *bent* on their deliberate deceit and defiance, then He reluctantly leaves them to their chosen fate. He first diagnoses their problem, then renders His just judgment. Persistence in their sin and attachment to their idols is their malady. "For Israel is stubborn like a stubborn calf; now the Lord will let them forage like a lamb in open country" (Hos. 4:16). If His people insist on having their way like an untamed calf, then He would let then fend for themselves, unprotected like vulnerable lambs. And if His people's way of life is rebellion and their disloyalty is their obsession, He then leaves them to their own ways. "Ephraim is joined to idols, let him alone. Their drink is rebellion, they commit harlotry continually. Her rulers dearly love dishonor" (v. 17).

There should be no presumption here concerning how God deals with those who deliberately defy His will. We cannot presume that, no matter what, He will always be found or will always be near. Notice the word "while" in Isaiah 55:6. "Seek the Lord while He may be found, call upon Him while He is near." The clear implication here is that the time comes when God may not be found or be near. Contrary to popular belief, there is a limit to God's mercy and His striving with sinful humanity. That is why the idea of divine probation makes sense. And probation is not only a point in time at the end, but also a continuous process. Our decisions today serve as important factors in determining our destiny. "In every age there is given to men their day of light and privilege, a probationary time in which they may become reconciled to God. But there is a *limit* to this grace. Mercy may plead for years and slighted and rejected; but there comes a time when mercy makes her *last plea*. The heart becomes *so hardened* that it ceases to respond to the Spirit of God. Then the sweet, winning voice entreats the sinner

71

no longer, and reproofs and warnings *cease*" (*The Desire of Ages*, p. 587; italics supplied).

Conditional Pardon

God's love is so misunderstood and abused in our day, that it becomes a convenient excuse for all sorts of wilfulness. It is claimed that God's love is so great that He forgives rebels without any conditions. The overemphasis on God's unconditional love, free choice, and mercy can embolden the unconverted to persist in sin with impunity. It is rationalized that whatever evil is committed does not matter anyway, for God is so generous in His love that He will overlook any transgression. This flippant attitude toward God's love and obedience to His law sets a dangerous example before others. For "Of all the sins that God will punish, *none* are more *grievous* in His sight than those that *encourage others to do evil*" (*Patriarchs and Prophets*, p. 323; italics supplied).

Thus God's love is "degraded to a weak sentimentalism, making little distinction between good and evil. God's justice, His denunciation of sin, the requirements of His holy law, are all kept out of sight" (*The Great Controversy*, p. 558). This is one of Satan's great deceptions. His ardent desire is to keep people from loving obedience to God. His tactics are represented by the saying, "Misery loves company," and he is desperately trying to have as many join him in his misery. He knows he is doomed and defeated, and his time is short. Throughout history he has deceived many by enticing them to oppose obedience to God's law. Such do not only want to do their own thing, but at the same time feel entitled to God's favor.

This is how the evil one wants people to view God's love, mercy, and forgiveness: "Satan deceives many with the plausible theory that God's love for His people is so great that He will

Salvation from Sin

excuse sin in them . . . The *unconditional pardon* of sin *never* has been, and *never* will be. Such pardon would show the *abandonment* of the principles of righteousness, which are the very foundation of the government of God. It would fill the unfallen universe with consternation . . . The so-called benevolence which would set aside justice is not benevolence but *weakness*" (*Patriarchs and Prophets*, p. 522).

But what is so amazing about God is that even after we stubbornly hold on to our idols, He still creates an opening for hope and reconciliation. Ephraim, who is so attached to his idols as to life itself, should hopefully question his defiance and reconsider: "Ephraim shall say, 'What have I to do anymore with idols?'" (Hos. 14:8). He and all the prodigal sons and daughters can still come to their senses and repent, even though they deliberately reject God's plan for them. The door of mercy is still open if they choose to humble themselves and repent. He graciously promises: "I will heal their backsliding, I will love them freely" (v. 4). And the last verse of Hosea ends on this hopeful note that God's repentant people recognize that "the ways of the Lord are right; and the righteous walk in them, but transgressors stumble in them" (v. 9).

True Repentance

Let us go back to the parable of the prodigal son, and contemplate his sincere repentance and the abiding love of the father: "I will arise and go to my father, and will say to him, 'Father, I have sinned against heaven and before you, and I am no longer worthy to be called your son, make me like one of your hired servants.' And he arose and came to his father. But when he was a great way off, his father saw him and had compassion, and ran and fell on his neck and kissed him" (Lk. 15:17-21).

Christ's Way to Restoration

A story is told of a moving account of a prodigal son and his family that took place during World War I. The parents were loving and godly, and provided their son with a good home life. When he reached his teens he decided to leave home, rebelling against them, and rejecting the family values he was raised with. Years passed by without any kind of contact, yet his parents never stopped thinking of him and praying for him. Their son was always on their minds and in their hearts. Later on he was drafted into the military to be trained and to be sent into the war zone, risking his life. The home that he left years earlier was located close to the railroad tracks.

Learning at his deployment that his train was to pass by their home, he telegraphed his parents about his deployment, and that his train would pass right by them at a particular time. He concluded his message by asking them for a small favor–to tie a white handkerchief to the mail box so he would know, as his train passed by, if they still loved him and thought of him. Days later, when his train passed by, he was so pleasantly surprised to see not only the mail box completely draped in white, but the entire house! Apparently, their hearts were so stirred by his request that they used anything white they possessed, plus what they managed to borrow from their neighbors.

To show us His great love, our heavenly Father sent His only Son to shed His precious blood for each one of us. His crimson blood splashed across the heavens, crying out from the soaked earth of Golgotha: My prodigal son and daughter, come home!

Discussion Questions

1. How do we, advertently or inadvertently, make it easy or difficult for others to sin?

Salvation from Sin

2. People sometimes focus on what is fun not on what is right. Why is that? What difference does it make to focus on either?

3. We often think of God's grace as His unmerited favor. But how does such grace empower us to resist and overcome evil? How does God's grace implant enmity against evil in the heart?

4. In our modern world, intolerance of evil conduct is sometimes considered worse than the evil conduct itself. Why is this so? What difference does this make?

5. What does Ellen White mean by using such terms as "mistaken kindness," and "dangerous presumption"? How does the understanding of these terms help us in counseling others wisely?

6. What are the active and passive virtues, as referred to in this chapter? When can we use these virtues most effectively, and why?

7. "Ephraim is joined to idols, let him alone" (Hos. 4:17). Why would our loving God say this? Explain what Ellen White meant when she asserted that there is a "limit to His grace"?

CHAPTER FOUR

Deliverance from Death

I was struck by a gripping scene of a life-and-death struggle shown on television. It was definitely a heroic deliverance from the jaws of certain death. A herd of water buffalos was being stalked by a pack of hungry lions. The camera then zoomed in as the chase was on, revealing that the lions were after a baby buffalo running beside its mother next to a river bank. One lion suddenly leaped onto the juvenile buffalo, grabbing it by the throat, skidding into the river. Instantly the waiting jaws of a crocodile locked onto the buffalo's hind legs. The struggle was savagely fought over this hapless and doomed victim, pulling it in opposite directions and seeming to rip it into pieces. Finally, the lion prevailed over the crocodile, and proceeded to strangle the poor thing to death. The other lions were waiting close by to share in the meal.

Seeing the desperate struggle of its baby from a distance, the mother bravely confronted the pack of vicious lions. Charging the lion, she bravely plowed into him with her long horns, sending him flying in the air. And with the help of other buffalos, who now joined her, she chased all the lions away. The incredible thing was that the baby buffalo actually survived, got up on its feet, and followed its mother to safety.

The Mighty and the Terrible

The Creator gave this maternal instinct to the buffalo to rescue her baby caught in the jaws of death. If this mere beast fought so bravely for her baby, how much more is our heavenly Father eager and able to deliver us from the jaws of eternal death! But even though the devil still "walks about like a roaring lion, seeking whom it may devour" (1 Pet. 5:8), Christ our defender is greater than our adversary . The "mighty" and "terrible" in Isaiah 49:24, 25 can aptly represent such a roaring lion. "Shall the prey be taken from the mighty, or the captives of the righteous be delivered? But thus says the Lord: 'Even the captives of the mighty shall be taken away, and the prey of the terrible be delivered; for I will contend with him who contends with you, and I will save your children."

One cannot help but compare the mother buffalo contending with the "mighty" lion and the "terrible" crocodile, and God's fierce contention to save our children. It is heroic to fight mighty and terrible beasts, especially when they are holding on to their prey. A lion is most dangerous when hungry and when challenged for its prized prey.

Today I heard on the news a moving account of the paternal impulse to deliver a child from danger and death. A father and mother hiking with their five-year old son were suddenly attacked by a mountain lion. Without any warning, the lion pounced on their child, grabbing him by the head and running off in the brush. Instinctively the slightly-built father, ignoring the danger to his own life, took off to do battle with the hungry lion. This brave dad fought off the lion singlehandedly, snatching his little boy from the jaws of death.

Christ's Way to Restoration

Humanity is in the death grip of the most vicious and determined lions, Satan himself. He is voracious enough to devour all of humanity. But Christ the "Lion of Judah" is more than a match for him. Christ pursued him all the way to the cross, snatching his human prey out of his deadly jaws. He defeated death with His own death. This heroic divine rescue forever resolved the biggest dilemma of the human race: death.

Destined to Die

Let us face this stark fact of human existence that we are born to die. Death is insolvable, unavoidable, and hopeless. It is the result of sin of which every one of us is guilty of. For "all have sinned and fall short of the glory of God" (Rom. 3:23). And what is sin? "Whoever commits sin also commits lawlessness, and sin is lawlessness" (1 Jn. 3:4). All this lawlessness leads to certain death: "For the wages of sin is death" (Rom. 6:23). Here we see naked justice without mercy, which dispenses death for sin. This inflexible law of cause and effect is what Hosea and Paul talk about: "They sow the wind, and reap the whirlwind," and "whatever a man sows, that he will also reap" (Hos. 8:7; Gal. 6:7).

In Hinduism there is only naked and exacting justice, devoid of any forgiveness or mercy. It is taught that human beings are in the grip of the cyclical law of *karma* and *samsara*. That is to say, the works of karma, good or bad, will result in the exacting outcome of samsara of future reincarnation. The depressing thing about this is that there is no way out of this vicious cycle. Though in the Christian world we are not worried about the law of karma, yet we worry about our final demise. The anxiety about mishaps and the uncertainty of life, the worry about catastrophic illness, the concern about getting old, and the dread of becoming incapacitated in a nursing home somewhere. The bottom line of all this angst is the inevitable and steady march toward death.

In their attempt to ignore their impending fate, people avoid talking about their age, try to hide their wrinkles and gray hair, and even subject their sagging bodies to the scalpel of cosmetic surgeons. Even the language they use to refer to this unpleasant subject reflects their inner fear. They say, he "passed away," or "he departed" instead of simply saying, he died. In funeral homes there are "slumber" rooms. Even after people die, make-up artists use all their skill to make the deceased look good. One time a woman came into the "slumber" room to comfort her widowed friend. Looking at the body, all made up, and trying to say something uplifting, she blurted out: "He really looks great in there." To that the widow quickly responded: "He doesn't look great, he looks dead."

The Great Exchange

If we consider human destiny, without any saving mercy but only stark justice, we are all doomed. Absolutely no one can deal with this inescapable and dire outcome except God Himself. No holy angels nor unfallen beings can rescue people from this hopeless pit. They do not possess life, and therefore cannot give it. They only borrow it from its Source, the life Giver. Life immortal is not something inherent in any creature, unfallen or fallen; for only God inherently possess it. "He who is the blessed and only Potentate, the King of kings, and Lord of lords, who alone has immortality . . ." (1 Tim. 6:15, 16). Only the Son of God, who volunteered to give His life for a condemned and doomed humanity, defeated our death with His death. "The *possessor* and *giver* of eternal life, Christ was the *only one* who could conquer death" (*Testimonies*, vol. 6, p. 231; italics supplied).

Christ's Way to Restoration

How was Christ's plan of deliverance from death implemented? The answer is found in what I like to call the "great exchange." Christ devised an eternal plan of substitution to rescue fallen humanity from death. You see, the two lethal liabilities that confront us are sin and death; and Christ's unique advantages are righteousness and life. As the Lord of righteousness and the Prince of life, He was willing to exchange our liabilities for His advantages. Justice was not slighted in the least, for in His vicarious death justice and mercy kissed each other. He paid dearly with His own blood for the infinite demands of the law. We sowed the wind but Christ reaped the whirlwind. Therefore, through His substitutionary death He is able to be merciful and just, and to justify those who receive Him in their hearts.

We all like a good bargain when shopping. It feels good to get the best quality for the least price. We have the greatest of all exchanges in what Jesus offered: receiving the absolute best without any cost to us. Of course, He paid the ultimate price through His shed blood, and it is all ours if we receive it by faith and live it by the power of the Spirit. Paul describes such a great exchange this way: "For He [God] made Him [Christ] who knew no sin to be sin for us, that we might become the righteousness of God in Him" (2 Cor. 5:21).

From eternity Christ is righteousness and life, and from Eden lost sin and death have been humanity's ordeal. But when justice kissed mercy in Christ's sacrifice, an awesome substitution took place. Christ vicariously took sin from us unto Himself, and replaced it with His own righteousness in us. He also took death away from us and replaced it with His own life. "Therefore, as through one man's offense judgment came to all men, resulting in condemnation, even so through one Man's [Christ's] righteous act the free gift came to all men, resulting in justification of life" (Rom. 5:18).

Deliverance from Death

Thus this glorious outcome: the removal of sin and deliverance from death are substituted with righteousness and life. Here is the most balanced and complete statement about this grand substitution found in *The Desire of Ages*. "Christ was treated as we deserve, that we might be treated as He deserves. He was condemned for our sins, for which He had no share, that we might be justified by His righteousness, in which we had no share. He suffered the death which was ours, that we might receive the life which was His" (p. 25). When this becomes actualized in the converted heart through the Spirit, then we move into a new life of being dead unto sin and alive unto Christ in righteousness.

Living Righteously Not Licentiously

To walk with Christ in righteousness is the life march to the kingdom, but to walk apart from Christ in disobedience is the death march to destruction. He wants us to choose life and reject death, and this is possible because sin, the cause of death, has no power over us. "For sin shall not have dominion over you, for you are not under law but under grace" (Rom. 6:14). God's gifts of grace and law were intended for different purposes. We are saved by His grace to obey His law. We are saved from the dominion of sin and death by God's grace that enables us to live righteously, never licentiously. Through Christ's death we become dead to sin and self, and that is why we are liberated from their tyranny to live righteously. God never intended that living under grace should ever become a license to sin but liberation from it. That is what Paul had in mind when he rhetorically asked: "What then? Shall we sin because we are not under the law but under grace?" His emphatic answer: "Certainly not!" (Rom. 6:15).

Christ's Way to Restoration

The apostle Paul vigorously severs any connection between sin and grace. How could we dishonor Christ's sacrifice and disregard His grace to liberate us from sin by living in it! Again he raises another rhetorical question that he decisively answers: "What shall we say then? Shall we continue in sin that grace may abound? Certainly not! How shall we who died to sin live any longer in it?" (Rom. 6:1, 2). In Christ we have died to sin and self so that we may walk with Him in the newness of life. "Through Satan's temptations the whole human race have become transgressors of God's law, but by the sacrifice of His Son a way is opened whereby they may return to God. Through the grace of Christ they may be enabled to render obedience to the Father's law" (Patriarchs and Prophets, p. 338).

This enabling grace of Christ, which frees us from the bondage of sin and its death penalty, comes with rich and life-long blessings. When we die to sin and self and live unto Christ and righteousness, we become secure and strong in our Christian walk. This results from a joint sacred experience with Jesus. Paul starts with Christ's experience: "For the death that He died, He died to sin once for all; but the life that He lives, He lives to God." Then he connects it with our experience: "Likewise you also, reckon yourselves to be dead indeed to sin, but alive to God in Christ Jesus our Lord" (Rom. 6:10, 11). The converted Christian is someone who experiences the dynamics of two selves: the old self and the new self.

Walking According to the Spirit

A certain church member wanted to share with me an exciting idea about the pre-advent judgment that brought relief to him. The Bible says that "there is now no condemnation," he explained, "and if there is no condemnation now, then there is no fear of the judgment, and no worry about death." That sounded

Deliverance from Death

like great news to me. Desiring to see if he had a full picture of what Paul intended, I proceeded to read him the whole text in Romans 8:1. "There is therefore now no condemnation to those who are in Christ Jesus, who do not walk according to the flesh, but according to the Spirit."

This church member discovered that he was focusing only on the first part of the text, neglecting the second part with its three essential conditions. There should be no worry about condemnation leading to death if we do the following:

1. *We must be in Christ.* There must be this living and transforming union with our Lord. Just as He described it in John 15:4, 6 when He said to His disciples: "Abide in Me, and I in you. As the branch cannot bear fruit of itself, unless it abides in the vine , neither can you, unless you abide in Me." Moreover, "If anyone does not abide in Me, he is cast out as a branch and is withered; and they gather them into the fire, and they are burned."

2. *We must not walk according to the flesh.* Certainly walking according to the old sinful self, that is supposed to have died, disconnects us from Christ the Vine. And branches that are disconnected from the vine wither and are condemned to burning.

3. *We must walk according to the Spirit.* We must choose either to walk with Christ or the flesh, but not both. Simply and logically put: We cannot serve two masters, and if we try we become conflicted within, and end up serving the master of the flesh. "No one can act like a worldling without being carried down by the current of the world. No one will make any upward progress without persevering effort. He who would overcome must hold fast to Christ. He must not look back, but keep the eye ever upward . . . Satan is playing the game of life for

Christ's Way to Restoration

your soul. Swerve not to his side a single inch, lest he gain advantage over you" (*Testimonies*, vol. 6, pp. 147, 148). Of course, we should never try to gain the victory by ourselves, lest we be overcome by our wily enemy. But the regenerating power of the Holy Spirit enables us to be transformed, and leads us to experience the reality of the gospel. Christ works His will through the Spirit to transform our lives and make us Christlike. "For the law of the Spirit of life in Christ Jesus has made me free from the law of sin and death" (Rom. 8:2).

Christ's Death Alone Gives Life

What does it mean in our everyday lives to be dead to sin and self-centeredness, and alive unto Christ and His righteousness? When we reckon that our old self is dead and our new self is hid in Christ, scorn, denouncement, and persecution do not upset us because our old self is *dead*. Like the saying goes, it is useless to beat a dead horse. But how does the new self handle such attacks? It is handled through the strength acquired by being in Christ, and the security that comes from walking with Him. When the new self is alive unto Christ, then whatever attack is leveled at us is absorbed by Jesus Himself. Let's not worry about the dead self, because it is dead. Let's not be anxious about the new self walking with Christ, because He is its shield and fortress. Instead of squandering our precious energy on deflecting Satan's attacks, let us dedicate our new selves to faithfully walk with Jesus and serve Him with all our hearts.

The death and life of Christ is the only hope for doomed humanity. His plan offers the only resolution to the sin and death problem. This was Christ's emphasis throughout His ministry. Notice how He pointed to His broken body and spilled blood as the only hope. "Most assuredly, I say to you, unless you eat the flesh of the Son of Man, and drink His blood, you have no

Deliverance from Death

life in you." And Jesus went on to say: "Whoever eats My flesh and drinks My blood has eternal life, and I will raise him up at the last day" (Jn. 6:53, 54).

Satan was keenly aware that only Christ's shed blood could rescue the human race. He was diametrically opposed to the prospect of Christ's death and the consequent liberation from sin's bondage and penalty. He relentlessly fought the prospect of the Seed of the woman [Christ] crushing his head and redeeming the human race. At every juncture in human history, he desperately endeavored to impede the coming of the Redeemer. He well knew that humanity was under condemnation and eternal death, and the only solution to this inevitable fate was the gift of Christ's life. He was keenly aware that Christ was on a divine mission to wrestle the dying world from his grasp with His own death.

He was struck with fear and anger at the birth of Jesus, knowing that this was the fulfillment of the promise of redemption. Through the cruelty of king Herod and the unbelieving Jews, he repeatedly tried to destroy His life before the cross, and thus snuff out any hope of salvation. On pages 15 and 16 of *The Desire of Ages*, we see how progressively Satan was filled with dread and anger at the coming the Redeemer:

1. "That the Son of God should come to this earth as a man filled him [Satan] with amazement and with apprehension. He could not fathom the mystery of this great sacrifice."

2. "From the time when He was a babe in Bethlehem, He was continually assailed by the evil one."

3. In the "councils of Satan it was determined that He was to be overcome . . . The forces of the confederacy of evil were set upon His track to engage in warfare against Him, and if possible to prevail over Him."

Christ's Way to Restoration

4. For Satan, the warfare against Christ's mission was a matter of eternal destiny, a life and death struggle. He was determined to fight it furiously to the bitter end. "Satan saw that he must either conquer or be conquered."

5. This life and death struggle against the Redeemer was so crucial to him that he had to personally take full command. "The issues of the conflict involved too much to be entrusted to his confederate angels. He must personally conduct the warfare. All the energies of apostasy were rallied against the Son of God. Christ was made the mark of every weapon of hell."

Did Satan Want Christ to Die?

There seems to be a paradox in Satan's approach to Christ's mission of salvation. He did not mind for Him to die a normal human death; but never to die the vicarious death of the Lamb of God on Calvary's altar. In the wilderness of temptation, he tried to subtly talk Jesus out of dying for the human race. He offered instead to give Him back this lost world if He would just bow before him.

"Why make it so difficult for yourself," Satan may have reasoned with Jesus. When he showed Him a panoramic view of the whole world from a high mountain, he tried to entice Jesus to bargain with him. He may have said to Him to take the easy way out and recover the world without sacrificing His life for it. "Again, the devil took Him up to an exceedingly high mountain, and showed Him all the kingdoms of the world and their glory. And he said to Him, 'All these things I will give You if You will fall down and worship me'" (Matt. 4:8, 9). "Now when the devil had ended every temptation, he departed from Him until an opportune time" (Lk. 4:13).

Deliverance from Death

At the rebuke of Christ, the devil left reluctantly only to try again. And an opportune time did arrive to discourage Jesus from going to the cross through His loyal disciple Peter. We need to keep in mind that sometimes the devil uses our best friends to discourage us from following God's plan, and often they do this inadvertently. For our close friends tend to have such a great influence on us. That is why our ultimate trust must always be God's solid word. In this particular instance recorded in Matthew 16:21-23, Jesus tells His disciples that He must suffer and be killed to save humanity. Peter inadvertently began to discourage Him from His plan to die; and he even took Him to task. "Then Peter took Him aside and began to rebuke Him, saying 'Far be it from You, Lord; this shall not happen to you!" Listen to Christ's severe response to, knowing that the source was not Peter but Satan himself: "Get behind Me, Satan! You are an offense to Me, for you are not mindful of the things of God, but the things of men." It is telling that Christ used the same words of rebuke in addressing both Satan and Peter: "Get behind Me, Satan!" Obviously, He was rebuking Satan who was speaking through Peter.

Watch the deceiver's subtle temptation through Peter in spite of Peter's love–albeit misguided– for His Master. "Satan was trying to discourage Jesus, and turn Him from His mission; and Peter, in His blind love, was giving voice to the temptation . . . His instigation was behind that impulsive appeal." Then notice the similarity of the two temptations issuing from the same source: "In the wilderness, Satan had offered Christ the dominion of the world on condition of forsaking the path of humiliation and sacrifice. Now he was presenting the same temptation to the disciple of Christ" (*The Desire of Ages*, p. 416).

It is amazing that shortly before Christ's rebuke of him as a mouthpiece for Satan, the same Peter was used as a mouth-

Christ's Way to Restoration

piece for God. At the same locale of Caesarea Philippi, Peter was heartily commended and then sternly rebuked. He declared through his powerful testimony that Jesus was "the Christ, the Son of the living God" (Matt. 16:16). And Jesus commended him with an unequivocal blessing: "Blessed are you, Simon Bar-Jonah, for flesh and blood has not revealed this to you, but My Father who is in heaven" (v. 17).

Judas' Strategic Gamble

Satan wasn't through with Jesus yet. During the Passion week, he used Judas in his attempt to discourage Jesus from dying on the cross. In betraying Christ, Judas did not want Him to die but live to establish an earthly kingdom over Israel. And Judas' strategy was quite similar to Satan's: Jesus should not have to die but live and establish an earthly kingdom over the whole world. In both instances, Judas and Satan would get the credit and the homage for their selfish deed. In the chapter on Judas, in the book *The Desire of Ages*, pages 716-722, we may glean several insights into the progression of his deception and rebellion. Recall to mind our discussion of Lucifer's deception and rebellion in heaven as we look at Judas' similar experience in relating to Jesus.

1. Judas' strategy was that Jesus would be forced to declare Himself an earthly king over Israel. In fact Judas "had marked out a line upon which he expected Christ to work . . . Judas wanted more aggressive warfare" (p. 718). He acted as a self-appointed political campaign manager, so to speak. Christ was never into politics, but Judas was immersed in it. He was so arrogant to think that he could manage and control Christ's life and mission. He viewed Him as the best choice for king of Israel, but thought that He was politically naive, lacking the right touch.

Deliverance from Death

2. Judas was self-serving in trying to advance Christ's career. He was looking out for his own good in the future new government. "The prospect of having a high place in the new kingdom had led Judas to espouse the cause of Christ" (*Ibid.*).

3. In his speculative mind, Judas had hoped to coerce Christ into becoming king at the feeding of the five thousand. "Judas was first to take advantage of the enthusiasm excited by the miracle of the loaves. It was he who set on foot the project to take Christ by force and make Him king" (*Ibid.*, pp. 718, 719). When his hopes were dashed he became bitter, and resented any mention of Christ's spiritual kingdom.

4. In his pride and self-centeredness he employed deception, subtlety, selfish ambition, and pretended conscientiousness. He twisted Christ's words and attributed to them the wrong intentions. He claimed that "his principles and methods would differ somewhat from Christ's, but in these things he thought himself wiser than Christ" (*Ibid.*). Jesus perceived that Satan was channeling his evil influence through Judas in order to influence his fellow disciples. Christ, referring to Judas, said to His disciples: "Did I not choose you, the twelve, and one of you is a devil?" (Jn. 6:70).

5. Judas calculated that he had made a "sharp bargain in betraying his Lord." If on one hand Christ was destined to die, then his betrayal would make no difference. But if on the other hand, He was destined to be king, then He would deliver and declare Himself king over the nation, and be grateful to Judas for pushing Him to do what He was too timid or too naive to do (*Ibid.*, P. 720).

6. Judas studied carefully Christ's past precedents of escaping when He was in a tight spot. He miraculously escaped a few times when He was on the verge of being stoned, and the

one time when the mob was ready to push Him over a cliff. If He did not allow Himself to be captured or killed before, Judas may have reasoned, then why would He allow Himself to die now, considering this was the most hideous kind of death. That is why when he betrayed Jesus he said to the mob, "Hold Him fast" (Matt. 26:48), expecting Him to reveal His miraculous power of breaking loose from His fetters. Judas did not imagine that when He betrayed His Lord he was betraying Him unto certain death. (*Ibid.*, P. 721).

7. When it finally dawned on Judas that Christ was going to the cross after all, a terrible panic gripped him. He could not fathom seeing that his blind and contrived betrayal would send Christ to the cross. In terrible anguish, Judas admitted his sin of betraying innocent blood. "Eagerly grasping the robe of Caiaphas, he implored him to release Jesus," but to no avail. Then he made a dash to Jesus, prostrating himself at his feet, and begging Him to escape just one more time. In pity, Jesus replied that for this precise purpose He had come to die for the sinful world.

So far Jesus had borne long with him, patiently and lovingly reaching out to him without subjecting him to public censure. In loving his rebellious disciple, He loved him to the very end. Jesus knew well the scheming heart of His disciple. He knew that he "did not repent; his confession was forced from his guilty soul by an awful sense of condemnation, but he felt no deep, heartbreaking grief that he had betrayed the spotless Son of God." He became so enmeshed in his sin, and so entangled in his lies that he became firmly welded to his rebellion. He and his sin became one, so in the end Christ had to let him go. What a tragic ending for Judas! Too little too late. He could not imagine Jesus dying the worst death, and in utter despair, bordering on insanity, he went and hung himself (*Ibid.*, pp. 721722).

Deliverance from Death

In the Garden, Satan fought savagely Christ's determination to give up His life to save the world. Satan tried his utmost to block through any means His path to Calvary. When the destiny of the human race was hanging in the balance as Jesus struggled with this colossal decision, Satan wished that Christ would not drink the cup. But when He made the heroic decision to drink the cup by submitting to His Father's will, Satan knew he was now defeated. Thus he shifted his battle plans to unleash his hellish forces to make the death of Jesus most painful. His awful suffering, the jeers from the mob, the abandonment of His own disciples, and the crushing burden of carrying the sins of the whole world did not deter His mission to die. And when He uttered the words, "It is finished," committing His spirit into His Father's hand, Satan's defeat was assured.

However, Satan never gives up in spite of the fact he knows he is defeated. He tried by any means to keep Jesus in the grave, but no power could do so. He was resurrected by the glorious power of His Father, and seen by many Roman soldiers. And the only way Satan could deal with this transparent truth was to use the Jewish leaders to buy the false testimony of the soldiers. He was desperate to cast doubt on the clear evidence of Christ's resurrection, in order that sinners might not believe and be delivered from death. And he continues to carry forth his lies about Christ's glorious resurrection to this day.

Judas and Lucifer: Similarities

It is quite revealing to notice the similarities between Lucifer and Judas, and how Christ labored lovingly and patiently with them both, knowing all along the intents of their hearts, and their eventual downfall. Their wrong choices led them to defy their Benefactor with impunity. Thus Judas launched a controversy of evil against good, reminiscent of the great controversy in heaven. Jesus referred to Judas as a devil in John 6:70, depicting him as He depicted Satan himself. Here are some comparisons and observations for our consideration:

1. Both carried meaningful names with a great message. "Lucifer" comes from the Latin which literally means, "light bearer." The name "Judas" is a Greek transliteration of the Hebrew *Yehudah*, which literally means, "Let Him [God] be praised." Both meanings reveal the great potential God had for these two: to shine forth with the light of God's truth, and to fill the air with praises to Him.

2. Both lived out the opposite of the wonderful messages their names conveyed. One diffused darkness rather than light, the other brought disparagement instead of praise.

3. Such darkness and disparagement eventually led them to become devils. Remember what Jesus said of Judas in John 6:70. "Jesus answered them, 'Did I not choose you, the twelve, and one of you is a devil?' He spoke of Judas Iscariot, the son of Simon."

4. They both fought to the bitter end Christ's way to save the fallen race through His death.

5. Both Lucifer and Judas were leaders entrusted with great responsibility, admired and respected by the unsuspecting angels and disciples.

6. Both used subtle deception to carry out their rebellious schemes. They utilized religious camouflage and spiritual veneer to hide their conniving and restless rebellion. To the very end, the angels and the disciples suspected neither of them.

7. They both were massive liars. There is no truth in Satan, for "he is a liar and the father of it" (Jn. 8:44). One of Judas' lies was that he pretended to care for the poor while stealing

from the poor. "This he said, not that he cared for the poor, but because he was a thief, and had the money box; and he used to take what was put in it" (Jn. 12:6). Also they both twisted Christ's words, attributing to Him wrong motives in order to fit their own deceptive schemes. Lying is so hideous to God, especially when it becomes persistent. It is almost impossible to deal with it because it is so deliberate, calculating, and confusing. By necessity it destroys trust in the deceptive person; and it is so unsettling that one can never be sure of anything that person says.

8. They were both traitors. Christ had his Lucifer in heaven and his Judas on earth. Treason was their hallmark in spite of their intimate relationship with Him. Despite his relentless love and longsuffering, they still betrayed Him. Jesus knew that Judas was going to betray Him, yet He still washed his feet and ate with him. After Judas ate the bread Satan entered him, leading him to walk out into the darkness to do his treacherous deed. That was to fulfill, according to Jesus, the psalmist's Messianic prophecy: "Even my familiar friend in whom I trusted, who ate my bread, he lifted up his heel against me" (Ps. 41:9; compare Jn. 13:18).

Historically the above prediction may refer to Absalom's wanton treason toward his loving and trusting father. But in a specific way, it was to apply to Judas, Christ's familiar friend in whom He trusted. In fact, Jesus still called him "friend" even after he betrayed Him with a kiss (Matt. 26:50). Jesus trusted Judas and Lucifer, and they became His familiar friends closely bonded to Him. Yet in spite of all that, they bit the hand that fed them, so to speak. To lift one's heel against a trusted friend, suggests gross ingratitude and betrayal. The heel used in this manner represents baseness and betrayal. And in this context here it is used to imply being insulted, kicked, or made to stumble.

Christ's Way to Restoration

9. They both thought they were wiser than Jesus. Lucifer thought he had a better plan for his fellow angels and the universe, and Judas imagined he had a better plan for his fellow disciples and Israel. And they were so arrogant to think that they could succeed in bending Christ's will to theirs. They were so overconfident to try to manipulate and manage Christ, telling Him what to do. They were ruthlessly and blindly ambitious even to try to usurp Christ's rightful position.

10. Finally they both "hung" themselves: Satan's defeat at Christ's death, to be consummated in the lake of fire. Crazed and despondent, Judas rushed out and hung himself from a tree. Jesus died for the right cause of delivering doomed humanity from death. Judas died and Satan will die for the wrong cause of plunging humanity into death. Not only will the devil, the author of death, die but death itself will be no more. The apostles John and Paul personify death as an enemy to highlight its sure destruction. "Then Death and Hades were cast into the lake of fire. This is the second death" (Rev. 20:14). Then Paul affirms that death is the final enemy to be destroyed. "The last enemy that will be destroyed is death" (1 Cor. 15:26). Praise God! Christ destroyed death with His death.

Loved unto Death

This chapter was introduced by a horrific story of rescue from certain death. How a father risked his life to save his son from the jaws of a hungry mountain lion. The conclusion here will be about another rescue account from certain death. But this rescue story is about a daring father who was killed in the process of defending his twelve-year old daughter.

The father, mother, and their young daughter were enjoying a leisurely stroll together one afternoon in a nearby park. The daughter seemed secure walking between her dad and mom

Deliverance from Death

while some teenage boys were following behind. All of a sudden, the boys grabbed the hapless girl and began to abuse her while dragging her into the nearby woods. The father never left her sight. And although outnumbered, he fought tenaciously to rescue his precious daughter from this vicious assault. Some of the guys turned on him, and started beating him mercilessly until he died. Also his poor daughter was raped and murdered. The mother was suddenly left alone to mourn the terrible loss of her family. What a terrible tragedy!

There is a much happier ending to Christ's rescue mission of humanity from the jaws of death. In the process of rescuing us, He was mocked, abandoned, flogged, tormented, and was finally killed in the worst way imaginable. All of this was done to take our place and deliver us from eternal death. Yet the good news is that the grave could not keep Him down. He rose again for you and me, defeating death with His death. Now, as we serve a risen Savior; let us walk with Him in this world until He comes again.

Christ's Way to Restoration

Discussion Questions

1. You read the rescue stories of the fearless mother buffalo and the daring father. How do such accounts help us to trust in our heavenly Father's absolute commitment and ability to save us? What hungry and roaring lions are striking fear in us right now? What can we do about it?

2. Why was Christ uniquely qualified to deliver us from eternal death? Why couldn't a perfect angel or an unfallen being accomplish this same mission?

3. How can sin be rendered powerless in our lives? What does it mean to be dead to sin? In Romans 8:1, Paul writes: "There is therefore now no condemnation . . ." What does the rest of the text say about the conditions we must meet in order for us to be liberated from such condemnation?

4. Satan did not want Christ to die, and he fought vigorously to accomplish such goal. Why?

5. Judas' risky strategy was to manage and control Jesus. Why did he think that he knew better than Jesus how to execute His own mission?

6. In what ways do we go ahead of Christ sometimes, and then wonder why He is not following? What is the remedy for this wilfulness?

Deliverance from Death

CHAPTER FIVE

Living the Law of Love

One of my students came back to school after the summer break, anxious to tell me an exciting idea about salvation. When he arrived at my office, I curiously inquired about the good news he was about to share with me. I really had no idea what he had in mind, but he said it was about our love for Christ. I told him that was a good subject I greatly appreciated. I waited for him to tell me what it was that he had in mind. He said smilingly, "Love Jesus and do as I please." "That is it in a nutshell," he asserted. "It is really a win-win situation. Jesus is happy, and I am happy." He further explained. This way he could be free from any restraint, so that he could live by grace, not having to worry about obedience. Such notion freed him, he claimed, to enjoy worldly pleasures, knowing that Christ's unconditional love would cover his many sins.

Christ's Good Pleasure

I told my good student that I liked the first part of his catch phrase, but I questioned the second part. The problem was the "I" in "do as I please." I simply wanted to replace the "I" with the "He" so that it would read, "I love Jesus and I do as *He* pleases."

Living the Law of Love

We do not live to please self but to please the Savior. That does not mean we are against pleasure, but the genuine pleasure we seek is that which results from pleasing Jesus. "Work out your own salvation in fear and trembling," Paul encourages the believers, because "it is God who works in you both to will and to do for His good pleasure" (Phil. 2:13).

There is godly pleasure which Jesus gives us as we faithfully follow Him. But the emphasis here is not on our own pleasure but His. As we wholeheartedly submit ourselves to Christ, He converts us, motivates us, and empowers us to do according to *His* good pleasure. Through Jesus God wants to "make you complete in every good work to do His will, working in you what is pleasing in His sight" (Heb. 13:21). So when we truly love Jesus we become His new creation, rejoicing to please Him in all things. It is through His divine power that we are enabled to submit our will to His, and to do what is pleasing in His sight.

Even our Lord did not seek His own pleasure, so why should we? "For even Christ did not please Himself" (Rom. 15:3). Genuine pleasure is not something we chase after, but it is the natural outcome of loving obedience to God and service to others. Christ's utmost pleasure was to please His Father. What is our highest pleasure? If indeed we desire the greatest pleasure in life, then pleasing our Savior is the perfect answer. This is what Jesus said: "And He who sent Me is with Me. The Father has not left Me alone, for I always do those things that please Him" (Jn. 8:29).

The spirit embodied in the catchy slogan that my student adopted—claiming to love Jesus and yet doing his own thing—is not uncommon. It is becoming fashionable today because it fosters an easy and cheap religion. It camouflages self-centeredness in love talk. But genuine love is not something we talk, it is something we walk. It is not some words we profess with our mouth, but a transforming reality we possess in our heart. That is the example which Christ showed us, and if we are serious about being His disciples then we emulate His example. Look how far Jesus walked love: from the glory of heaven to the gore of earth. Paul puts it this way: "And walk in love, as Christ also has loved us and given Himself for us, an offering and a sacrifice to God for a sweet-smelling aroma" (Eph. 5:2).

There is no room for mere pretension here if we truly desire to be radical disciples of Christ. If we genuinely long to be Christlike, we are to be intimately attached to Him. Sooner or later, mere outward profession will reveal there is no inward possession. How do we know for sure, especially in our own lives, what is mere profession and what is real possession? "There is a huge difference between pretended union and real union with Christ. A profession of the truth places men in the church, but this does not prove that they have a vital connection with the living Vine. A rule is given by which true disciples may be distinguished from those who claim to follow Christ but have no faith in Him. Those who are fruit-bearing, and those who are fruitless. (See *Testimonies*, vol. 5, pp. 228, 229).

Jesus was free of all pretension, for He walked love all the way to Calvary not to satisfy Himself, but to sacrifice His life to save sinful humanity. This kind of love exacted an inestimable price: His blood. When we love Him with all our hearts we want to please and obey Him in all things. We want to offer ourselves as living sacrifices of loving obedience and service to Him. This is what the love of Christ looks like: it is clothed in trust and obedience. Notice how John tells us what love is, and then links it directly and emphatically to obedience. "For this is the love of God, that we keep His commandments. And His commandments are not burdensome" (1 Jn. 5:3).

Christ's Yoke and Burden

The words "not burdensome" remind us of what Jesus said about His yoke: "My yoke is easy and My burden is light" (Matt. 11:3). The Pharisees' yoke of legalism was so crushing that the strong-willed among the Jews languished under its heavy burden, and the others like the publicans simply gave up, drifting into hopelessness. Jesus came to relieve people of such oppressive yokes and heavy burdens, and offer a different alternative: His way of life. And if they submit to His way and walk with Him, His yoke will be pleasant and His burden will be light. The term "yoke" represents an implement of service, a joint cooperative effort to lighten a load, a symbol of submission for discipline and training.

To sit at the feet of Jesus, and learn His ways is what it means to be yoked to Him. He Himself is a mighty yet gentle yoke bearer, and He calls us to join Him so that He would render our yoke bearable and pleasant. All things become possible, easier, and more pleasant when we join forces with Christ. Thus in submitting to Him and following His ways, we become like Him in doing His will and reflecting His character. Of course, His character is revealed in His law of love that "yokes" us close to Him, and places a hedge of protection and security around us. Without the yoke of His law of love, we would wander aimlessly following our own proclivity, doing our own will not His.

As you noticed from our discussion, there is a connection between the yoke we take with Jesus and the keeping of His law. "We are to take upon us His yoke, that we may be coworkers with Him. The *yoke* that binds to service *is* the *law of God*. The great law of love revealed in Eden, proclaimed upon Sinai, and in the new covenant written in the heart, is that which *binds* the human worker to the *will of God*. If we were left to follow *our own inclinations*, to go just where our will would lead us, we should fall into Satan's ranks and become possessors of his attributes. Therefore God *confines* us to His will, which is high, and noble, and elevating . . . He [Christ] said, 'I delight to do thy will, O My God: yea, Thy law is within My heart.' Ps. 40:8" (*The Desire of Ages*, p. 329; italics supplied).

I grew up on a farm in the Bible lands, and I had seen many times farmers yoking oxen to plow their fields. What used to amaze me was that these patient yet powerful beasts of labor would be so submissive and disciplined, plowing hardened soil for days on end. I remember one farmer yoking his small donkey next to his strong ox when his other ox fell sick, and proceeded to plow. I remember seeing the ox moving ahead of the donkey, doing most of the heavy pulling. In our life journey, we are yoked with Jesus, pulling ahead toward the kingdom. We are weak and He is strong, but we become strong in His strength as we embark on life's journey with Him. And all along, as we cooperate with Him, He does most of the heavy lifting. Encouragingly, He tells us that He loves us, and if we stick with Him we will make it.

Our Good Pleasure

I cannot go further without looking again at my student's slogan, "Love Jesus and do as I please," from a different angle. The perspective of sanctification I am going to address was not at all in my student's mind. However, I wanted to redirect his mind to see things in a different light. I explained to him that Christian liberty is not license. The grace God entrusts us with is not there to encourage us to disobey. How could that be the case if the born-again Christian is dead to sin and alive unto Christ?

Living the Law of Love

We simply cannot indulge ourselves in what we are dead to. Yet it is true that if we are wholeheartedly converted and walking with Jesus as Enoch did, then naturally what pleases Him, pleases us, and what pleases us pleases Him. This is what it means to have the mind of Christ, and to be daily transformed into His likeness. We love what He loves, and hate what He hates. Like Him, we love righteousness and hate unrighteousness.

My student realized afresh that there is more to our walk with Jesus than he originally thought. Our emphasis ought to be: no tolerance to sinful practices but always empowerment to grow in sanctification. This is what it means to be totally submissive to Christ, covered with His robe of righteousness: we live His life. Ellen White aptly explains it this way: "When we *submit* ourselves to Christ, the heart is *united* with His heart, the will is *merged* in His will, the mind becomes *one* with His mind, the thoughts are brought into *captivity* to Him; *we live His life*. This is what it means to be clothed with the garment of His righteousness" (*Christ's Object Lessons*, p. 312; italics supplied).

The only correct way we may view the idea of loving Jesus and doing as we please, is in the context of our heart obedience to Him. We reach this intimate union with Him as we live His life, that we spontaneously obey Him with all our heart. "All *true* obedience comes from the heart. It was *heart* work with Christ. And if we *consent*, He will so *identify* Himself with our thoughts and aims, so *blend* our hearts and minds into *conformity* to His will, that when obeying Him we shall be but carrying out *our own impulses*. The will, *refined* and *sanctified*, will find its *highest delight* in doing His service. When we know God as it is our privilege to know Him, our life will be a life of *continual obedience*. Through an *appreciation* of the character of

Christ's Way to Restoration

Christ, through *communion* with God, sin will become *hateful* to us" (*The Desire of Ages*, p. 668; italics supplied).

Therefore when Christ's pleasure spontaneously becomes our pleasure, then this is not some sort of frivolous notion we entertain, but a serious experience of sanctification. To such who are in Christ, walking with Him in loving obedience, Romans 8:1 becomes applicable. There is no condemnation to them because they are "in Christ Jesus, who do not walk according to the flesh, but according to the Spirit." Notice how Paul makes his idea crystal clear by the use of the negative and positive: do *not walk* according to the *flesh*, but *do walk* according to the *Spirit*.

Abidance and Obedience

Does not Romans 8:1 harmonize with the previous two statements quoted above? There are conditions involved in our Christian walk. There are fruits that reveal the truth in our hearts. Review with me the emphasized stipulations therein which has to do with our submission to Christ:

1. Our hearts become united with His heart.

2. Our will becomes merged in His will.

3. Our Mind becomes one with His mind.

4. Our Thoughts become captive to His thoughts

5. Therefore, we live His life in our lives.

The second statement from *The Desire of Ages*

1. Christ's obedience to His Father was heart work, so too should be our obedience to Him.

2. If we submit ourselves to Him as He submitted Himself to His Father, then:

Living the Law of Love

a. He will so identify Himself with our thoughts and goals.

b. He will so blend our hearts and minds to conform to His will.

c. Therefore, gloriously when obeying Him we shall be but carrying out our own impulses.

d. Hence, our sanctified will finds its highest delight in pleasing and serving Him.

3. When we know and love God with all our being, then:

a. Our life for Him will be a life of continual loving obedience.

b. Sin will become hateful to us through appreciation and communion with Christ.

The apostle John resonates with the idea of linking our lives with Jesus in love, obedience, and service. So we ask him to tell us more about the love of God. How do we know for sure that we love God? "By this we know that we love the children of God, when we love God and keep His commandments" (1 Jn. 5:2). Such authentic love to God propels us to keep His commandments, and moves us to extend this love to others.

There is something clear and balanced about this in John 14:15–the indivisible union of loving Jesus and keeping His commandments. "If you love Me, keep My commandments." I like the conditional "If "in Christ's injunction, because it implies that if we do not keep His commandments, we do not really love Him. To truly love Christ is to trust and obey Him. This is one integrated, balanced, and complete package. The balance is there in Christ's words, and we must always keep it there to avoid the pitfalls of extremism. If we emphasize love without resulting obedience we drift toward nominalism; and on the other hand, if we emphasize obedience without love we slide into legalism–neither is a happy or fruitful prospect.

The apostle John, whom Christ kept on loving, does not only provide us with a balanced definition of genuine love, but he also instructs us on how to maintain that love. Again, Jesus shows by example how to follow Him in this regard: "If you keep My commandments, you will abide in My love, just as I have kept My Father's commandments and abide in His love" (Jn. 15:10). To obey, then, is to abide. The careless spirit of doing our own thing, simply because of our freedom of choice, leads to dislodgement not lodgement in Christ. Our focus on pleasing Christ and not self provides us with a hedge of security and protection to help us in our continual abidance in Christ.

Many who claim to be disciples of Christ find themselves pulled toward, what I would call, the *sweetness* of the gospel but not the *substance* of the gospel. Often they are attracted to the sweetness of Christ's salvation, but not to the substance of His lordship. But He is inseparably and irrevocably both: He is the Savior we love, and the Lord we obey. It is like a jam sandwich. If we only eat the sweet jam it becomes intolerable, and if we merely eat the dry bread it becomes unbearable. It is a good idea, then, to keep the whole sandwich together: the sweetness of the jam and the substance of the bread.

Law: Relationship, Liberty, and Love

As was alluded to earlier, keeping the commandments is a profound expression of our love for God, plus they provide us with a hedge of security from evil . But some say that keeping them is restraining and even enslaving. They wonder why John would tell us that "the commandments are not burdensome" (1 Jn. 5:3). In carefully studying the preamble to the Decalogue in Exodus 20, we notice that God saved His people from Egypt's

Living the Law of Love

bondage before asking them to obey. In other words, they were not called upon to keep the law in order to be saved, but they were saved to keep the law. Keeping God's commandments was always meant to be a manifestation of our love and gratitude for His salvation.

In the Decalogue's preamble (Ex. 20:2), God says: "I am the Lord your God who brought you out of the land of Egypt, out of the house of bondage." In these first words which God proclaims to His people, He reminds them of the special *relationship* He has with them. He does not say, "I am the Lord God," but "I am the Lord your God." The possessive pronoun "your" implies relationship and belonging. He is not just a God to them, rather He is *their* God; He belongs to them and they belong to Him. And in this framework of relationship, He grants His people freedom. The idea of freedom is inferred in the context. To bring them "out of bondage" implies to bring them *into* freedom, the opposite of bondage.

After the preamble, we notice that the commandments begin with verse three and conclude with verse seventeen. These commandments can be summarized by one word: love. And according to Jesus, this love extends to our God and to our neighbor—forming the two great commandments. "And on these two commandments hang all the Law and the Prophets" (Matt. 22:40). God calls upon us, His people, to love Him with all our hearts, and to love our neighbors as ourselves in the preamble of relationship and freedom. Thus the Decalogue and its preamble can be summed up in three words: relationship, freedom, and love. God establishes a relationship with us as a Person, and a belonging to Him as a family. Then He liberates us from the bondage to sin's slavery, so that we may love Him with all our being and others as ourselves. There is no hint here of enslavement, but only freedom to trust, love, and obey.

Christ's Way to Restoration

When Jesus said that the second great commandment is "like" the first one, He meant that both of them originated from the same Source. Genuine love to our neighbor springs forth from our love relationship to God. Living one of these commandments is not truly possible without living the other. Some try to love God without loving their neighbors, and tragically love neither. Some others focus on loving their neighbors but not their God; however such human-centered love dries up, and they too end up loving neither. The second commandment grows out of the first and reinforces it in real life. "Both these commandments are an expression of the principle of love. The first cannot be kept and the second broken, nor can the second be kept while the first is broken. When *God has His rightful place* on the throne of the heart, the *right place* will be given to our *neighbor*. We shall love him as ourselves. And *only* as we love *God supremely* is it possible to love our *neighbor impartially*" (*The Desire of Ages*, p. 607; italics supplied).

What Is Self-Love?

I do not want this opportunity to pass without adding a clarifying note about the two great commandments of which Jesus spoke. The need for this clarification is that I see more and more Christians using this reference to highlight the idea of self-worth to the extreme. Let us review the context of this text in Matthew 22:34-40. A lawyer asked Jesus to tell him which was the greatest commandment. Notice that he asked only about *one* commandment. Jesus answered his question directly: "You shall love the Lord your God with all your heart, with all your soul, and with all your mind" (v. 37). Then Jesus went beyond informing him about the first commandment, and volunteered to tell him about the *second* great commandment. "And the second is like it: You shall love your neighbor as yourself" (v. 39).

Living the Law of Love

These two great commandments are in essence about God and neighbor: Love your God and love your neighbor. Each one was given with a stipulation or provision. Love your God. How? With all your being. Then love your neighbor. How? As yourself. There is no third great commandment of "Love yourself" as some claim, because Christ did not give such. He limited Himself to give only two. Simply put, Christ presented no third commandment to love self in order to love God and neighbor. The proper and best way to love self is to focus on God's love to us and our reciprocal love to Him. Then from that position of love and security anchored in Christ, we can altruistically love our neighbor.

You see, we do not start by focusing on loving self, but on God's love and on the costly price Christ invested in us–His precious blood. Imagine, our value is worth the life of Christ! Genuine love of our neighbor and proper love of self is a byproduct, a natural outcome of our awesome love experience with God. The danger is that there is, in our humanistic world, so much focus and obsession with self under the guise of self-love or self-worth. Such focus leads to self-centeredness, which can lead to self-entitlement, which can further lead to self-worship or narcism. It is a telling sign that the more our society becomes obsessed with the idea of self-worth, the less of it is experienced. This is because the only source of real self-worth is Jesus. That is why we know in our innermost beings that the most awesome thing to experience is God's great love, the inestimable value He invested in us, and that such an experience will spontaneously overflow to people around us.

John, the apostle of love, who experienced Christ's reciprocal love first hand, encapsulated this idea when he wrote: "By this we know that we love the children of God, when we love God and keep His commandments" (1 Jn. 5:2). This is such a profound, proper, and reciprocal concept of love. For the *proof* that we love our neighbors *is* loving Him and keeping His commandments. Loving God from the heart results in the fruitful obedience to the commandments. When we lovingly obey God in keeping the first four commandments, we are moved to love our neighbor in the last six. The determinative question we must ask here is: do we truly love God with *all* our hearts? Do we love Him more than anyone else or any thing else? Do we put Him first before our cherished children or our service to Him?

Anyone or anything, no matter how wonderful, if such usurps the priority of God in our lives, such becomes our idol. This includes our spiritual activities and successful service to others. There are so many noble distractions from Christ, but there is only one priority attraction: Christ. And from Him, the Source, flows out His love into our hearts, and in turn it flows out of our hearts toward others. "Many who bear the name of Christians are serving other gods besides the Lord. Our Creator demands our supreme devotion, our first allegiance. Anything which tends to abate our love for God, or to interfere with the service due Him, becomes thereby an idol" (*Signs of the Times*, Jan. 26, 1882).

The Law Is Eternal and Universal

The principles embodied in the Decalogue were not temporarily devised for the children of Israel in the wilderness, but they were eternal principles governing the entire universe. They are as eternal and unchangeable as God Himself, for they are the perfect reflection of His character and the bedrock of His government. To the holy angels, obedience to God's law in their inward being was natural and spontaneous, for it sprung up from a grateful and joyous heart. To them obedience was a delight not a drudgery, something loving not legalistic. "When Satan rebelled against the law of Jehovah, the thought that there was a law came to the angels almost as an awakening to something unthought of . . . Obedience is to them no drudgery. Love for God makes their service a joy" (*Mount of Blessings*, p. 109).

This reminds me of a fellow student who resided in the dormitory during his four years of college. While the dean of men struggled correcting the frequent infractions of some dorm residents, this student never had any trouble with the rules. The dean would painstakingly explain the handbook of regulations to the insubordinate ones, and deal with all their complaints and excuses, while this young man was not even aware such a regulation book existed! Because of the way he viewed things, and the right choices he made in life, doing the right thing came naturally. For him, compliance with dorm rules was not a burden but a blessing. This is just a small glimpse of how the angels must have felt in heaven. Doesn't this remind us of what the psalmist said about God's law? "I delight to do Your will, O my God, and Your law is within my heart" (Ps. 40:8).

What about our first parents? Did they know about God's law before sin entered the world? God's law had existed from eternity, and to eternity it will continue to exist. It was there even before the angels and man were created. It was planted in their hearts by the Spirit, yet it was attuned to their circumstances. "Adam and Eve, at their creation, had a knowledge of the law of God. It was printed on their hearts, and they understood its claims upon them. The law of God existed before man was created. It was adapted to the conditions of holy beings; even angels were governed by it. After the fall the principles of righteousness were unchanged . . . And as it has existed from the beginning, so will it continue to exist throughout the ceaseless ages of eternity" (*The SDA Bible Commentary, EGW Comments*, vol. 1, vol. p. 1104).

Christ's Way to Restoration

Isn't it narrow minded, then, to think that God's law was intended only for the Jewish people? It is an expression of His character, and therefore as eternal and immutable as He is. His holy law applies to His entire universe, not just one people, or even one world. Never compromising its changeless and eternal principles in the least, God adapted it to reach our human race. But some think that this ancient law does not apply to them, or if it does it has to fit their own feelings and convictions. They also claim that the principles of God's law are not existentially real to them unless they can subjectively experience them. It is obvious that the U.S. Constitution is objectively real, even if some say it is not, simply because they do not personally experience it. Similarly, God's law is real regardless of what any one thinks about it.

To the Law and Testimony

Then there are those who feel impressed that the Lord has definitely convicted them to think a certain way or do a certain thing. I chuckle when I think of a young man who claimed that he was strongly convicted by God to marry a certain young woman. Now it happened that I knew both of them as my students. It was funny to watch how determined he was to persuade her of his conviction, only to drive her away. She was certainly sure that God convicted her of no such thing, insisting that the young man never talk to her again. This incident may seem facetious to us, but more and more persons are attributing their unreliable subjective convictions to God.

Christ warns that we need to be vigilant, for many deceptions will be perpetrated against His followers, and human opinions will make His word of no effect. So our only safety is found in this solid injunction: "To the law and to the testimony! If they do not speak according to this word, it is because

Living the Law of Love

there is no light in them" (Isa. 8:20). The Hebrew word for "law" is *torah*, which refers not only to the Decalogue and the Pentateuch, but more inclusively to all the revealed will of God in the Scriptures. Isaiah draws us closer to God's reliable word, and away from false and unreliable human opinions. God's true word must always be our unwavering standard for truth, and our unifying common denominator. The light of His word is the undimmed "lamp to my feet and a light to my path" (Ps. 119:105), the psalmist testified. When we relish the sweetness of God's word which gives us true wisdom, then we "hate every false way" (v. 104).

I had the opportunity to counsel a family about a crucial decision the son was about to make. That decision, according to his parents, was to adversely and profoundly impact his entire life. Without delving into all the details of the family conflict, I shared with them Isaiah 8:20, requesting that they put all their different opinions aside and adhere to God's standard; for it is indeed the just equalizer and the fair common denominator. Unfortunately, when the son realized that God's word went contrary to his impending decision, he balked at heeding it. His lame defense was that even if he were going contrary to God's counsel, his right to choose made his impending decision justifiable, regardless of consequences. After all, he said, he prayed about it and felt impressed that God was pleased with what pleased him.

I am sure that if people are humble enough to subject their personal convictions to the unifying standard of God's word, His light of truth and harmony would shine upon them. How I wish more people would take seriously this cautionary counsel, and realize that anything that is not in accordance with God's word is darkness: "In the face of the most positive commands of God, men and women will follow their *own inclinations*, and then *dare to pray* over the matter, to prevail upon God to allow them to go contrary to His expressed will. *Satan* comes to the side of such persons, as He did to Eve in Eden, and *impresses* them. They have an exercise of mind, and this they relate as a *most wonderful experience* which the Lord has given them. But *true experience* will be in harmony with natural and divine law" (*Counsels on Health*, p. 109, italics supplied).

The Beauty of Balance

Satan's specialized skill is to take what is in harmonious balance and twist it into disharmony and disequilibrium. The longer I live the more I appreciate the word *balance*. A balanced approach is God's safeguard against Satan's enticements to extremes. A good example of this extremism is the misconception of the divine and human role in salvation. What is the role of faith and works? Some say that good works have no bearing on our salvation, because Jesus did all the work for us. In other words, there is nothing they can do because Jesus did everything. The Bible avoids such confusion by providing us with ample evidence for proper balance. Let us consider Paul's approach to salvation. He explains: "For by grace you have been saved through faith, and that is not of yourselves; it is the gift of God, not of any works, lest anyone should boast. For we are His workmanship, created in Christ Jesus for good works, which God prepared beforehand that we should walk in them" (Eph. 2:8-10).

Let us review carefully the proper and logical balance in this passage. First, he properly starts with the gift of God's grace for salvation that is appropriated by faith. Second, this is not done by *our* own works but by *His* own gift of grace. Third, such a gift of grace appropriated through faith makes us new creatures in Christ Jesus. Fourth, the purpose of this new creation in Jesus

Living the Law of Love

is to help us be fruitful in good works. But such fruitfulness is only possible through His new creation in us. Notice the proper use of these two words : "by" and "for." We are not saved *by* good works but *for* good works. We are saved *by* grace *for* good works. Fifth, we "should walk" in such good works in our everyday life.

Therefore, good works are natural and crucial as a result of God's re-creation by His grace. It was predestined before creation that God's grace must be followed by good works as proof of the fact. The "by" and "for" can also be expressed consecutively in two practical words: *root* and *fruit*. In other words, the *root* of our salvation by grace is necessarily followed by the *fruit* of our salvation in good works. This balance is built in God's eternal plan of our salvation, and cannot be compromised with. If the emphasis is only on the root and not the fruit, then cheap grace and careless living result. "The desire for an easy religion that requires no striving, no self-denial, no divorce from the follies of the world, has made the doctrine of faith, and faith only, a popular doctrine" (*The Great Controversy*, p. 472).

This is the imbalance Satan seeks to hide behind—a facade of superficial spirituality. For "It is not faith that claims the favor of Heaven without complying with the conditions upon which mercy is to be granted, it is presumption; for genuine faith has its foundation in the promises and provisions of the Scriptures" (*Ibid.*).

Sparks of Our Own Kindling

All too often religious activity is used to camouflage inward rebellion. Such religionists, who have *already* made up their minds about what pleases them, come to me under the guise of prayer to justify their wrong behavior. "Don't talk to me," one says, "I've already decided what I want to do." Or another says, "Go ahead and talk to me as much as you like, it won't do any good." Because all along such had resolved to be set in their ways, no matter what. The lamentable thing is that they claim to pray earnestly for God to close the door against their defiant decision, knowing well that His word had already closed it from the start. A subjective decision made so contrary to God's clear word. "I've already made my decision about this, and if God does not agree then He can stop me." How could God guide and bless someone who seeks His confirmation about a defiant decision? Tell me then, why would He stop someone who deliberately chooses to go against His clearly stated will revealed in His word?

The opposite of the above willful behavior is true: God never affirms what is against His word no matter how much we rationalize our independent conduct. We are to strive diligently to learn God's will and what pleases Him, and then prayerfully do it. God is not mocked, and it is an insult to His name to try to manipulate Him to fit into our ways under fake spirituality. Jesus' clear example was not to please Himself but to selflessly serve His Father and others. Here is the real danger: "The eyes, the ears, and the heart, will become unimpressible if men and women refuse to give heed to the divine counsel, and choose the way that is best pleasing to themselves" (*Sons and Daughters of God*, p. 175).

And here is the wise counsel: "We must not study to have our own way, but God's way and God's will." Otherwise such will "walk in the sparks of the fire they themselves have kindled, and the sure result is affliction, unrest, and sorrow, which they may have avoided if they submitted their will to God " (*Ibid.*). Fire represents God's presence, His word, His will, and His sovereignty. In kindling our own fire, we are trying to usurp God's place by setting up ourselves as the authority and arbiter of our

Living the Law of Love

decisions. Thus in dethroning the Lord in our decisions, we devise our own plans to walk in while all along rationalizing and presuming upon His support.

What fire are we kindling in this darkened world? Let us be clear on this crucial point: human kindling is always darkness, divine kindling is always light. It is when we insist on having our own convenient way regardless of consequences, that we rationalize the kindling of our disobedience. We strive to lower God's standards by the expedient standards of our own creation. We do not take seriously the "Thus says the Lord," but we try to get by with the least possible, cutting corners everywhere. Confronted by God's clear counsel that goes contrary to pleasing self, we try to work around it, minimize it, recast it, twist it, and all together rationalize it away. Thus undermining the clear counsel of God by our own kindling of self-centered notions. Therefore, "we are to make no compromise with the leaders of rebellion . . . We must have a firm determination to do the Lord's will at all times and in all places" (*Ibid.*, p. 215). Moreover, "Let it be written upon the conscience as with a pen of iron upon the rock, that real success, whether for this life or for the life to come, can be secured only by faithful adherence to the eternal principles of light" (*Testimonies*, vol. 7, p. 164).

A Way that Seems Right

Satan will intensify his deceptions in these last days, knowing that his time is short; therefore, it is indispensable that we join Jesus in resisting his subtle delusions. The tragic thing is that some of the brightest and best in our ranks will be deceived and fall away. That is what Jesus warned against in His eschatological chapter of Matthew 24, when He said that lying demonic agencies will endeavor to "deceive, if possible, even the elect" (v. 24). Haven't you heard some well-meaning Christians claiming that the Holy Spirit told them this or that? I myself have on several occasions. Ungrounded in the Spirit-inspired word of God, they fall prey to the deceiving spirits of devils. And they become so bewitched that they sincerely believe such lies and stubbornly act on them..

I had a sincere friend, who was sincerely wrong, telling me that he got the Spirit's gift of knowledge to advocate certain ideas. But when I discovered that such ideas were contrary to the word of God, I kindly told him so. How could it be possible that the Holy Spirit who inspired God's word would impress him with something diametrically opposed to it. The Holy Spirit is not divided against His own inspired revelation, I explained. But he insisted that such convictions felt so right and made him feel so happy and peaceful. At that moment the truth from God's word struck me like lightening: "There is a way that seems right to a man, but its end is the way of death" (Prov. 14:12).

In this age of doubt and unbelief, we must be devoted to God's way and not be deceived by the ways that seem right to us. If we do not pay heed to this, we are treading on Satan's enchanted ground as we face the final crisis. "Those who feel at liberty to question the Word of God, to doubt everything where there is *any chance* to be unbelieving, will find that it will require a *tremendous struggle* to have faith when trouble comes. It will be *almost impossible* to overcome the influence that *binds the mind* which has been *educated* in the line of unbelief, for by this course the soul is *bound* in Satan's snare and becomes *powerless to break the dreadful net* that has been woven closer and closer about the soul" (*Last Day Events*, pp. 68, 69; italics supplied).

Let us prayerfully contemplate these sobering insights about the great controversy that is being waged relentlessly in our own hearts. "Every variety of error will be brought out in the mysterious working of Satan, which would, if it were possible, deceive the very elect . . . The Lord has given men a rule by which to detect them: 'To the law and to the testimony: if they speak not according to this word, it is because there is no light in them.' If they belittle the law of God, if they pay no heed to His will as revealed in the testimonies of His Spirit, they are deceivers. (*The SDA Bible Commentary, EGW Comments,* vol. 7, p. 952).

Moreover, "They are *controlled by impulse and impressions* which they believe to be from the Holy Spirit and consider *more reliable* than the Inspired Word. They claim that every thought and feeling is an impression of the Spirit; and when they are reasoned with out of the Scriptures, they declare that they have something more reliable. But while they think that they are led by the Spirit of God, they are in reality following an imagination wrought upon by Satan . . . The Word of God is solid rock, and we may plant our feet securely upon it." (*Ibid.*).

Christ's Family

The apostle Paul warned the believers that after his departure two major attacks would be leveled against them: attacks from without and attacks from within. He predicts that in the future "savage wolves will come in among you, not sparing the flock." This is the expected frontal attack of persecution from outside. But here comes the more dismaying, deceptive, and dangerous kind: an attack from within. Paul continues his warning: "Also from among yourselves men will rise up speaking perverse things, to draw away the disciples after themselves" (Acts 20:29, 30). Here Paul echoes what His Master said concerning the subtle attacks from within. What Jesus warns about may sound so farfetched presently, but in reality it is so true. "And brother will deliver up brother to death, and a father his child; and children will rise up against parents and cause them to be put to death . . . and a man's enemies will be those of his household" (Matt. 10:21, 36).

Paul seemed quite exercised about this matter that he reminded them that for "three years I did not cease to warn everyone night and day with tears" (Acts 20:31). Then, what is the answer to such vicious and subtle assaults from without and within? How shall we face such demon-inspired onslaughts? The only answer is found in our supreme love and staunch loyalty to God and His word. Jesus said that when such attacks would take place, that we might lose family and friends, but He and His faithful people would become our loving and loyal family. But if we love the most dear to us more than we love Him, then when trouble comes we will be found wanting.

The criterion that Jesus presented for belonging to His spiritual family is based on loving obedience to God's will. Such a bond has to do with blood relationship through His blood shed on the cross, and a spiritual relationship through the Spirit shed in our hearts. Through His blood and Spirit we are enabled to do His will, in loving obedience. "But He [Jesus] answered and said to them, 'My mother and My brothers are these who hear the word of God and do it'" (Lk. 8:21). What constitutes this spiritual family bond with Jesus is not only hearing God's word with the ear, but also doing it from the heart.

Contemplate with me in these pertinent statements showing how Jesus views our spiritual kinship with Him and the heavenly family: "Those who accept Christ as their personal Savior are not left as orphans, to bear the trials of life alone. He receives them as members of the heavenly family; He bids them call His Father their Father . . . He has toward them an exceeding tenderness, as far surpassing what our father and mother has felt toward us in our helplessness as the divine is above the

Living the Law of Love

human . . . It was to redeem us that He became our kinsman. Closer than father, mother, brother, friend, or lover is the Lord our Saviour" (*The Desire of ages*, 327).

See how this divine kinship with us overflows to the members of His family on earth. This is what bonds our spiritual family on earth with our spiritual family in heaven: loving obedience to God's will. "And if we do hold the relation of kinship to Him, with what tenderness should we regard those who are brethren and sisters of our Lord! Should we not be quick to recognize the claims of our divine relationship? Adopted into the family of God, should we not honor our Father and our kindred?" (*Ibid.*).

This family on earth is intended to be a prelude, giving us a foretaste of the larger heavenly family above. Again, the same universal criterion: loving obedience to our heavenly Father through the shed blood of our elder Brother Jesus, "from whom the whole family in heaven and earth is named" (Eph. 3:15). The spiritual ties that bind us to our heavenly Father and to our fellow believers, through the blood of Christ, can be more solid and lasting than even earthly blood ties. Such family members are blessed because they are bonded in God's love and united around obedience to His commandments. This is what will prepare them to enjoy the universal family of God when Christ returns to take them home. "Blessed are those who do His commandments, that they may have the right to the tree of life, and may enter through the gates into the city" (Rev. 22:14).

Rendering loving obedience to our heavenly Father, and doing His will is the indispensable condition for joining God's family in heaven. We need to practice being faithful to God here in order to be loyal citizens there. The bottom line is that we must be safe to save, for the evil of rebellion will not rise up again. "Through obedience to the laws of Jehovah, the human family may become a united, happy family in the city of God. But there is no room there for those who have no regard for the will of the Lord ... To those who will live a life that is in harmony with the Father, Christ will impart the virtues of His life" (*Sons and Daughters of God*, p. 47).

This is the purpose of the gospel work in the heart: to restore us to the original state of trusting in God's will and obeying His law. This is indeed indispensable for our eternal happiness, and safeguard of universal order and harmony. God's ultimate goal is to inscribe His law on the tablets of our hearts, so that our transformed hearts would resonate with the heartbeat of Jesus. But here is the proving ground where by our fruits, not merely by our claims, we shall be known. God's plan for the gospel is "to unite the hearts of His followers in a spirit of universal brotherhood, through belief of the truth, and thus establish heaven's system of order and harmony in the family of God on earth, that they may be accounted worthy to become members of the royal family above. God, in His wisdom and mercy, tests men and women here, to see if they will obey His voice and respect His law, or rebel as Satan did" (*Ibid.*, p. 50).

Now is the time to be anchored in God and settled in His truth, that no matter what the future holds we will be strong and secure under His wings. Now is the moment to discard all things that compromise the priority of our relationship with Him. Listen to Christ's cautionary counsel: "He who loves father or mother more than Me is not worthy of Me. And he who loves son or daughter more than Me is not worthy of Me. And he who does not take his cross and follow Me is not worthy of Me" (Matt. 10:37, 38). The choice is clear that with such a loving and loyal relationship with Jesus we have nothing to lose and everything to gain, but without it we have everything to lose and nothing to gain. "For what profit is it to a man if he gains the whole world, and loses his own soul? Or what will a man give in exchange for his soul?" (Matt. 16:26).

My Way or the Highway

Loving obedience to God's law and testimony is what unites the earthly and heavenly family together. And in such union there is no discord but harmony, because Jesus is the head and we are the members of His body. There is a close, mutual, and indispensable cooperation all around. No member would say I am going my way, doing my own thing, regardless of the rest. Such willfulness results only in disunity and destruction. In this dynamic process there is no self-centeredness, but only Christ-centeredness and reciprocal altruism. We and the rest of the vast universe painfully know all too well the cataclysmic consequences of self-centeredness. Striving to be our own god brings about only chaos, anarchy, and death.

I once had an interesting conversation with one of my students about his academic work. He complained about his poor grade, so I invited him to my office to see if I could help him do better. I tactfully advised him to attend more regularly, take notes in class, and read the text book. He did not seem to take interest in my suggestion, and brushed it aside as that "stuff." He asserted that he would rather learn in his own way, doing his own thing. He hinted, as he left my office, that I should consider gearing my course requirements to fit what he liked. This incident in academic life reflects, on a larger scale, the prevalent moral and spiritual environment of today.

People say, yes I believe in God, yet at the same time they want to be their own gods. They claim that God is loving and does not judge or reprove anyone, but is pleased with what pleases them. This reminds us of what Lucifer wanted in heaven:

no restraint, doing his own thing, and even expecting God to be supportive of such independence. But our God is not an indulgent and permissive Father who is pleased with whatever makes us feel good. He is never in the least interested in raising His children to be spoiled, doing their own thing with impunity.

The spiritualism that originated with Satan is the clever counterfeit of true spirituality toward God. It is not only the false belief that the dead can speak to us, but the deceptive notion that we are our own independent gods, usurpers of Jehovah's prerogatives. "Spiritualism asserts that men are unfallen demigods; that 'each mind will *judge itself*'; that 'true knowledge places men *above all law*': that 'all sins committed are *innocent*'; for 'whatever is, *is right*,' and 'God doth *not condemn*.' . . . Multitudes are thus led to believe that *desire is the highest law, that license is liberty*, and that man is accountable *only to himself.*" (*Education*, pp. 227, 228; italics supplied).

We see, don't we, that such subtle deceptions, in the philosophies of the new age, post-modernism, existentialism, cheap grace, and universalism are making inroads into all levels of society, even churches. What is our sure shield and defense for our families, and the world around us in the midst of all this confusion? "Here is the only safeguard for individual integrity, for the purity of the home, the well-being of society, or the stability of the nation. Amid all life's perplexities and dangers and conflicting claims, *the one safe and sure rule is to do what God says*" (*Ibid.* p. 46; italics supplied).

Safe to Save

It is good news for the entire universe that "there is no room there [heaven] for those who have no regard for the will of the Lord. All who will may gain everlasting life, but they must gain it by accepting the law of God as their guide in this life instead

Living the Law of Love

of seeking to follow their own laws" (*Ibid.*, p. 47). Wasn't this the example Jesus set before us to follow? Yes, by fulfilling the law–obeying and living it out in His own life–He delighted in it, exalted it, and made it honorable. He testified that our love relationship to God leads us to obey His commandments and abide in His love, just as He did. "As the Father loved Me, I also have loved you; abide in My love. If you keep My commandments, you will abide in My love, just as I have kept My Father's commandments and abide in His love" (Jn. 15:9, 10).

In every type of training for any profession the determinative question is: will such a person become a competent physician, teacher, engineer, etc.? All the study, research, tests, and boards that are taken boil down to the above question. It is taken for granted that the certifying boards do not ignore requirements and skills in their evaluations, so that they would not unleash a bunch of incompetents on the unsuspecting public. This would endanger public order and welfare. Why wouldn't this apply to the spiritual realm where there is so much more at stake? This whole life is a course we take to train us to become good citizens of heaven, preparing us for eternity. And we are blessed with the most competent and loving Teacher along with the angels, His capable assistants, to help us succeed.

Shouldn't this be our first and foremost priority right now? Isn't this the time to let Jesus equip us for heaven? It is right now during this crucial and final period of Christ's ministry of intercession and judgment in the Holy of Holies. If we neglect Christ's ministry on our behalf and fail in our preparation, then it would be catastrophic. That is why our loving obedience to God's law and submission to His will is to be taken very seriously. "God's object in giving the law to the fallen race was that man might, through Jesus, rise from His low estate to be one with God, that the greatest moral changes might be manifested in his nature and character. This moral transformation must take place, or man would not be a *safe subject* in the kingdom of God; for he would raise a revolt" (*Sons and Daughters of God*, p. 50; italics supplied).

God loves the redeemed and unfallen beings to such an extent that He would never jeopardize their eternal security. He simply can never be that careless that He would slip in non-transformed persons who would become cosmic anarchists. Obedience to God's law that works by love is intended to fashion our lives to reflect His image in us. For example, it is a recognized fact that the United States Constitution is one of the most important legal documents ever fashioned by humankind. It is the highest law of the land designed to inspire, protect, and pull the American people to an increasingly higher level of citizenship. In abiding by its principles it helps elevate one to the highest levels of citizenship.

Heavenly agencies take our spiritual growth very seriously, because their primary mission is to prepare us in this world to live loyally in the world to come. "Here in this life is the testing, trying time. The angels of God are watching the development of character, and weighing moral worth. The whole question is settled in this, Is he obedient or disobedient to the commandments of God? Has the sinner been transformed in this world, through the merits of Christ, to an obedient servant, so that he is fitted to join the heavenly society?" (*Ibid.*).

Our loving obedience to God's law does not only prepare us to be safe citizens of heaven, but also to be safe here from Satan's delusions. By God's grace, if we live His law, we are protected from Satan. But if we carelessly separate ourselves from God through wilful disobedience, then we become vulnerable prey to Satan's attacks. Under the guise of promoting freedom, he

Living the Law of Love

undermines the need for God's law as something stifling and re-strictive. But what nation can survive without good laws? What institution would thrive without order and respect for author-ity? Jesus admonishes us to pray for and support civil authority, and He urges us even more so to obey God's law and respect His authority. Those who live in insubordination to God's will on earth would definitely show such insubordination in heaven, if given a chance.

Confidence in God and His Word

The devil has a heyday when some Christians, including intellectuals and theologians, think it is in vogue to sit in judg-ment on God's word, as with any other work of literature. They convey a low view of inspiration by which they can recast the Scripture, reconstruct it, and reduce its infallible authority, thus rendering its injunctions doubtful. They want to squeeze the Bible into their human way of thinking, regardless of the detri-mental effects on people's trust in it. This seems to make them feel superior in their attempt to make God's word inferior. There is a certain element of pride and arrogance in using their keen minds to question and quibble on the minors while overlooking the overarching biblical message of salvation.

"There is nothing that Satan desires more than to destroy confidence in God and in His word. Satan stands at the head of the great army of doubters, and he works to the utmost of his power to beguile souls into his ranks. It is becoming fashionable to doubt . . . Those who are unwilling to obey its requirements endeavor to overthrow its authority . . . There are many who seem to feel that it is a virtue to stand on the side of unbelief, skepticism, and infidelity . . . But having openly expressed un-belief, they feel that they must maintain their position" (*The Great Controversy*, p. 526). God has given us a preponderance of evidence to believe in, but He does not remove every possibility for our finite minds to question. We are free to focus on distrust, thus deepening distrust; or we can focus on trust, thus strengthening trust. "All who look for hooks to hang their doubts upon will find them. And those who refuse to accept and obey God's word until every objection has been removed . . . will never come to the light" (*Ibid.*, p. 527).

Our minds and hearts must now become fortified in God's solid word. Even if we are in the small minority, as long as we cling to a "Thus says the Lord" we will be safe. All of us will be severely tested, and "None but those who have fortified the mind with the truths of the Bible will stand through the last great conflict" (*Ibid.*, pp. 593, 594). Friends, family, pastors, theologians may line up unitedly against one genuine believer in the word, yet he would prevail. The whole world can rally against our implicit confidence in the word, what is that to us? We can confidently say with Joshua: "But as for me and my house, we will serve the Lord" (Josh. 24:15).

Especially nowadays when much of people's spiritual experience is so subjective, we need to anchor our faith in the objective truth of God's word. Will we stand firm when persecutors malign us, cast our words in the worst light, and misconstrue our good motives? Will we distrust the convincing evidence of our logic if it goes contrary to the standard of God's word? How do we prepare for such a terrible onslaught? "Only those who have been diligent students of the Scriptures and those who received the love of the truth will be shielded from the powerful delusion that takes the world captive . . . Are the people of God now so *firmly established* upon His word that they would not yield to the *evidence of their senses*?" (*Ibid.*, p. 625; italics supplied).

Living the Law of Love

I had my share traveling by air—on jumbo jets as well as on small propeller planes. I had a couple harrowing flights on the latter. Sitting by a window, I saw how the small aircraft struggled against the dense darkness, howling winds, torrential rain, blinding lightening, and the explosive thunder. The plane, its crew, and passengers were totally at the mercy of nature's wrath. What would a pilot do in such a confusing situation, when east seemed west, up seemed down, and high seemed low? I saw first hand how he piloted us to safety. He was totally focused on the instrument panel, while constantly communicating with the control tower.

The Bible is God's instrument panel for us to focus on as we sojourn in this stormy world. Constant communication with God's strong tower through prayer is our sure safety. Let nothing distract us from focusing on the sure guidance of His word, and let our prayers flow unhindered to His throne of grace.

Discussion Questions

1. "Love Jesus and do as I please." What does this mean? How does Christ's good pleasure converge with our good pleasure? What difference does this make in our spiritual journey?

2. Christ said His "yoke is easy" (Matt. 11:3). What does His easy yoke represent? What connection does this yoke have with our cooperation, submission, service, and obedience to God's law?

3. How does abidance in Christ lead to obedience to Him? What does the sweetness and the substance of the gospel represent? How does an unbalanced view of faith lead us to an easy religion?

4. How does this statement help us to trust and obey God's word? "In the face of the most positive commands of God, men

and women will follow their own inclinations, and then dare to pray over the matter, to prevail upon God to allow them to go contrary to His expressed will. Satan comes to the side of such persons, as he did to Eve in Eden, and impresses them" (*Counsels on Health*, p. 109).

5. How does the law in Exodus 20 relate to relationship, liberty, and love?

6. What criteria did Christ establish in order to belong to His family? What is the connection between belonging to the earthly family and to the heavenly family?

7. What does "safe to save" have to do with our moral transformation? Are we safe to save now?

8. To live on the "sparks of our own kindling." How does this relate to superficial spirituality?

9. Ellen White provides an uncommon definition for spiritualism: God does not condemn or judge, and sins committed are innocent. What do you think of this in the light of God's standards?

10. If anyone or any cause—no matter how dear or noble to us—usurps the priority of Christ in our lives, such becomes our god or idol. How does this idea impact our relationship with Christ and others?

Living the Law of Love

CHAPTER SIX

In Christ's Likeness

A little boy loved Jesus very much, and enjoyed hearing his dad and mom read Bible stories to him. Every day he invited Jesus to come into his heart and live there. This little disciple thought the world of Jesus, and considered Him as his best friend and hero. Developmental psychologists tell us that children at this young age take things quite literally, being incapable of thinking in abstraction or symbolism. Children are naturally interested in how they are growing. So one day he asked his father: "Daddy, how tall am I?" "Last time I measured, you were about three feet tall," his dad casually responded. As the boy stood by his dad, looking up and down at him, he wanted to know how tall he was. "I am about five feet ten inches," his response came back.

Apparently the reason why this curious boy was asking these questions was because he was trying to figure out how tall Jesus was. Finally the boy asked the question he was leading up to: "Daddy, how tall is Jesus?" Surprised, the father said that he was not exactly sure, but explained that because He was Jesus He must be quite tall, maybe six feet six inches, like a basketball player. The wheels started turning in the boy's head, and after a pause he seemed relieved about inviting Jesus to live in his heart. "Daddy, Jesus is so tall and I am so small, so He must always be sticking out of me!"

Increase and Decrease

What a sublime description of what it really means to be a genuine follower of Jesus. It is true, isn't it, that wisdom proceeds from the mouths of babes. No wonder Jesus said: "Assuredly, I say to you, unless you are converted and become as little children, you will by no means enter the kingdom of heaven" (Matt. 18:3). Oh to be a converted disciple with a childlike heart! With such an ongoing experience with the Jesus we so admire, how could we not become more and more like Him. As we examine our hearts, let us ask ourselves: What is "sticking out" of us today? Is it self, or is it the Savior? There is too much of self seen today and too little of the Savior. This troubled world needs no more of the sinful self paraded; but is in desperate need of the transforming power of Christ.

Even one of the greatest prophets realized this fact when he said this of Jesus and of himself: "He must increase, but I must decrease" (Jn. 3:30). It is a spiritual axiom that as more of self disappears the more of Christ appears, and vice versa. We live in a world where self-centeredness is the accepted and encouraged norm. People are increasingly looking out for number one, promoting and marketing themselves. The only possible way we can become Christlike is by dying to self, so that Christ may live in and through us. That is why I find myself praying more often these days that I may become nothing that He may become everything. It is when we uplift Christ in our lives, that He will draw many unto Himself (Jn. 12:32).

Christ's Way to Restoration

According to Acts 11:26, the disciples were first called Christians in the biblical city of Antioch. The question arises as to why were they called by such a name. The heathens of ancient Antioch were known for using derogatory nicknames, intended to ridicule an individual or taunt a group. Apparently, the followers of Christ were so passionate about Him, that He was constantly on their minds and on their lips. They were so ardently devoted to their Savior and Lord, that He dominated every aspect of their daily lives.

We all know of people who are obsessed with certain hobbies or activities, and when we see them that is all they talk about. One of my friends is crazy about playing golf, and every time I see him he bombards me with many details about this game, regardless of my lack of interest. He lives for the game in his waking hours, and at night he dreams about it. Some people are depicted as "workaholic" when they become addicted to their work. Their work dominates every aspect of their lives. Others get so excited in watching their favorite sporting events, that they seem oblivious to everything else. If we can become so caught up in these temporary pursuits, how much more passionate should we be about the eternal rewards of becoming devoted disciples of Christ!

The Highest Type of Man

To the early Christians, Christ was their life, their food and drink, and the air they breathed. They preached Him and taught about Him everywhere. So it was obviously easy to nickname them "Christians" –a special name to be taunted and honored by. They were branded with this stigma, but were honored by the insignia of being Christlike. Christ spiritually reproduced Himself in them as they resembled Him before others. So what does it mean to be called Christians in our day?

In Christ's Likeness

Here is an excellent definition: "For to be a Christian is to be Christlike. Jesus is a perfect pattern, and we must imitate His example. A Christian is the highest type of man, a representative of Christ" (*Evangelism*, p. 641). There are four important points to keep in mind. First, what does it really mean to be a Christian? It is to be *Christlike*. Second, how do we become Christlike? It is by imitating Christ's example.

Third, what difference does this make in one's life? It makes one a true representative of Christ. Fourth, what is the spiritual standing of such a true representative? Such a person is the *highest* type of humanity, the superb specimen of God's grace, and the excellent showcase of His transforming power.

How do we know for sure that we are *becoming* more Christlike? Is Jesus our favorite subject to share with others? Do we love Him more than anyone or anything else in the world? Do we catch ourselves thinking often of Him and how to please Him in all things? If the answers to these questions are in the affirmative, then we are becoming more like Christ. "Who has the heart? With whom are our thoughts? Of whom do we love to converse? Who has our warmest affections and our best energies? (*Steps to Christ*, p. 58). Again, if Jesus is the answer to these questions, then that affirmation is the undeniable proof that we are being fashioned into His likeness.

It is by beholding Christ that we become changed into His likeness. That is what Paul meant when he wrote to the Corinthian believers: "But we all, with unveiled face, beholding as in a mirror the glory of the Lord, are being transformed into the same image from glory to glory, just as by the Spirit of the Lord" (2 Cor. 3:18). God's face was unveiled in the face of His incarnate Son, and in beholding Him we behold the Father. We behold with no obscurity His glory, dimming all worldly glitter and reflecting the light of His character. God desires for each of us to be conformed to the image of His Son. His ideal for us is for His light to shine brighter through us as we continue to walk in the Spirit.

Here are more unmistakable indicators that we are, by His grace, becoming increasingly like Jesus: "If we are Christ's, our sweetest thoughts are of Him. All we have and are is consecrated to Him. We long to bear His image, breathe His spirit, do His will, and please Him in all things." When people become so consecrated to Him, "they will follow in His steps, reflect His character, and purify themselves even as He is pure. The things they once hated, they now love; and the things that they once loved, they hate" (*Ibid.*). God's transforming power propels them to love what Jesus loves, and to hate what He hates. What Jesus would say and do becomes the uppermost consideration in living out His life. "When Christ is abiding in the soul the fact cannot be hid; for He is like a well of water springing up into everlasting life" (*Sons and Daughters*, p. 311).

Spiritual Olympics

This week the Olympic games are on, so I take a break now and then from writing to see what is happening. What impresses me most is the long and arduous training the athletes subject themselves to. And all of this heroic effort does not guarantee any of them a medal. Most of them experience only the agony of defeat, and go home empty-handed. All this strain and struggle, resulting in only a few winners, is for a perishable prize and fleeting fame. It is amazing that in our spiritual Olympics, where the prize never perishes and the glory never fades, we neglect such a great and eternal salvation. And because of Christ, who has victoriously run the race before us, we can all be victorious, we can all go for the imperishable gold.

In Christ's Likeness

This greatly inspires me to do my utmost best to run life's race with Jesus, no matter what it takes. I find myself praying: "Dear Lord, You did your best and went for broke on the cross for me. So help me to follow Your example in going for broke as well. Help me never to forget that Your sacred head wore a humiliating crown of thorns on the cross, so that I would wear a glorious crown in heaven. I desire with all my heart to come after You, carry my cross and follow You to the end. Please seal and sanctify this sacred desire of mine with Your Spirit. All for Your honor and glory. Amen."

It is interesting to note that the athletes are eager to adopt or abandon any practice that will enhance their chance to win. No sacrifice is too great for them in order to reach their lofty goal. Their devoted fans and supporters are there with their placards and voices to cheer them on to victory. The apostle Paul describes this decisive spiritual race we are engaged in. Christ the victorious leader is leading the way, the heroes of faith and all of heaven are cheering us on. "Therefore we also, since we are surrounded by so great a cloud of witnesses, let us lay aside every weight, and the sin which so easily ensnares us, and let us run with endurance the race that is set before us, looking unto Jesus, the author and finisher of our faith, who for the joy that was set before Him endured the cross, despising the shame, and has sat down at the right hand of the throne of God" (Heb. 12:1, 2).

In this passage from Hebrews is found the secret for victory in Christ. All the ingredients for winning the prize of Christlikeness and eternal inheritance are there. Let us outline some important steps in this victory march:

1. Jesus is the victorious leader, prized athlete, and valuable coach. He sacrificed all on the cross for us, and will exert every

effort at His disposal to help us win. What is His vital function in this valiant race of destiny?

a. Jesus is the author and originator of our faith and salvation. He is the One who launches us on the right path to the kingdom of grace and glory. By living faith, He justifies and sanctifies us as we walk with Him.

b. He is the finisher or perfecter of our faith and redemption. We are to be confident of "this very thing, that He who began a good work in you will complete it until the day of Jesus Christ" (Phil. 1:6). He is totally committed to us as His reclamation project, using all His rich resources to complete it. For "He is also able to save to the uttermost" (Heb. 7:25), not partially or temporarily but completely and eternally. By living faith, He also sanctifies us as we continue walking with Him. "It is no longer I who live, but Christ lives in me" (Gal. 2:20).

c. He is our joyous warrior who braved the pain, endured the cross, and ignoring the shame for the joy of saving us. Christ's anticipation of companionship with the redeemed helped Him endure the worst agony and death. While embracing the crude cross, His eye was on the prize of the costly crown. All for us!

2. We are Christ's spiritual athletes in this race. What are we to do to persevere and not lose heart in the face of trials and afflictions?

a. We are, first of all, to continue looking unto Jesus. He has already won the race for each one who is willing to submit to and cooperate with Him. We are not competing against anyone but against self. We are to emulate His example in this race, as we see glimpses of victory ahead of us. The stark truth in this race confronts us with two unavoidable alternatives: look up and live, or look down and lose. Looking up helps in this spiritual race, as evidenced in the familiar words of this chorus: "Turn your eyes upon Jesus, look full in His wonderful face, and the things of earth will grow strangely dim in the light of His glory and grace."

b. The numerous "cloud of witnesses" are there not as jealous competitors or passive spectators, but loyal and active supporters, cheering us on to victory. They themselves are a sure proof of winning with Jesus, hence we ourselves may now have confidence in our victory, and then share in their triumph.

c. We are to be eager to divest ourselves of anything that may hinder our forward march with Jesus. What runners would not rid themselves of any impediment in the race! In the Olympics, it is amazing how meticulous runners and swimmers are, for example, in choosing their outfits. No tiny hindrance is allowed that would make a split-second difference in the final outcome. We should readily cling to our Savior and decidedly separate ourselves from sin. No fellowship is possible between the sinless Savior and those who cling to sin. We should even go to the extent of discarding any activity–good or bad–that obscures Christ's priority in our lives. He must be first and foremost, all in all.

d. Endurance is a must in this race. Without it evil enticements and snares will distract and derail us from running the victorious course with Jesus. We are in this race for the long haul, despite obstacles and setbacks, until Jesus comes again. Patience and perseverance must be our priority to stay the course that Christ has set before us.

The Highest Position

Christlikeness is the quintessence of the spiritual race in our journey toward the kingdom. The precise objective of the Scriptures is to conform us into the image of Christ, and to prepare us to live in restored Eden. There are two superlative phrases which highlight such a glorious purpose of restoration. The first has to do with the *highest position* in life, and the second with the *greatest recognition* in life. The first naturally leads to the second, as we shall see.

It is natural for people to covet a high position or status in whatever they do. They are proud of receiving a promotion in their career, and often they like you to know about it. There is this vacuum, this restlessness in the human soul, that longs to be satisfied. But there is no remedy found for this insecurity except in Christ. When we are emptied of self, and in humility submit to Christ, then we become totally content to be the pliable clay in the hands of the Master Potter, to be fashioned in His likeness. Then "we are *not anxious* to have the *highest place*. We have no ambition to crowd and elbow ourselves into notice; but we feel that *our highest place is at the feet of our Saviour*. We look to Jesus, waiting for His hand to lead, listening for His voice to guide" (*The Mount of Blessing*, p. 15; italics supplied). Sitting at His feet in absolute trust and submission, being at His total disposal, is certainly the highest position we may ever reach in life. Consequently, Jesus can accomplish His will in our lives unhindered.

What good news! We have *already* reached the highest position when we humbly sit at Jesus' feet to be fashioned after His likeness. This is the only way God can rid us of insecurity, anxiety, and prideful ambition. Liberated from such cumbersome burdens, we can invest our energy into loving and serving Jesus. With full assurance we can trust all to Him to guide us in the way He pleases. And what matters what others think? If we are solidly anchored in Christ, other issues do not loom as big anymore. If we are embraced by Jesus the King of the universe, who cares what others think about us?

Remember, when Mary in her devotion to Christ came to anoint His body for burial, she was severely criticized for her act of devotion (Mk. 14:3-9). But Jesus defended her against such a harsh attack, and affirmed her in describing her act as something good and beautiful. Notice that she did not need to defend herself, for she was sitting in submission at the feet of her Defender. There, Mary had discovered the highest position in her life. Furthermore, Jesus explained what He meant by saying that she had done something beautiful to Him: doing her part, doing what she could. It is so uplifting to know that when we faithfully do our part, it is good enough for Jesus. When we lovingly do our part, it may not be good enough for others or even for ourselves. But if it is good enough for Jesus, then it surely is good enough! As Christ's witnesses, the disciples' position "was the most important to which human beings had ever been called, second only to that of Christ Himself" (*The Acts of the Apostles*, p. 19).

The Greatest Recognition

The second phrase, the *greatest recognition*, naturally flows out of the first phrase, the *highest position*. It is natural for us to desire recognition for some outstanding achievement in our professions. For example, teachers want to have a reputation for their effectiveness in the classroom, preachers aspire to be noticed as mighty communicators of the gospel, physicians welcome the recognition that they are skilled in the healing arts. But our greatest recognition, as disciples of Christ, is for others to take notice that we have been with Him. And how do they notice this in us? Because of the tremendous transformation that occurs while sitting at the feet of Jesus. When the Jewish leaders perceived such transformation in these uneducated men, they were astonished and they recognized that they had been with Jesus, for they so resembled Him in their character.

Sitting at His feet and learning from Him for three and a half years, the disciples began to resemble Him in their ways. "When the disciples came forth from the Saviour's training, they were no longer ignorant and uncultured. They had become like Him in mind and character, and men took knowledge of them that they had been with Jesus . . . Continual devotion establishes so close a relation between Jesus and His disciple that the Christian becomes like Him in mind and character " (*The Desire of Ages*, pp. 250, 251).

A little girl was walking with her mother into a church. The stained-glass windows depicted Christ's disciples, and the sun's brilliant rays were shining beautifully through the windows. "Mommy, now I know what good disciples of Jesus are like," the girl said. "The light of Christ shines out through them." We are to be clearly recognized as the light of the world, reflecting His brilliance and dispelling the devil's darkness. "The light and love and power of an indwelling Christ shone out through them, so that men, beholding, marveled" (*The Acts of the Apostles*, p. 65). This is the greatest recognition we can ever receive! Oh Lord, I pray, that people will always recognize me as having been with You, even if every earthly recognition is taken away from me.

Characteristics of Christlikeness

What are the characteristics of being Christlike? If we have the opportunity to interact with Christlike persons, how would they come across to us? What does Christlikeness look like in the real world? These are some of the characteristics or qualities of being Christlike, presented here for our prayerful consideration.

In Christ's Likeness

1. **Selflessness.** A Christlike person is someone who is dead to self and alive unto Christ. Not self-centered but Christ-centered. All spiritual problems stem from self-centeredness. Self is so nurtured and alive that it needs to be excused, defended, and satisfied at any cost. We see ourselves and others not from the perspective of self, but from the Savior's perspective. Self becomes nothing to us so that the Savior may become everything to us. In fact, selflessness is God's effective antidote for self-centeredness.

2. **Submissiveness.** Lasting behavior change and character transformation is the direct result of submission to God's will and direction. The workable formula for Christlike transformation is outlined by Jesus Himself in Luke 6:40. "A disciple is not above his teacher, but everyone who is perfectly trained will be like his teacher." Christ focuses on two essential conditions to fashion us into His image: First, He is the expert trainer and transformer, and He knows exactly what it takes to mold us into His likeness. Second, we are the open-hearted and teachable trainees, placing ourselves totally at Christ's disposal, and letting Him have free reign to do as He pleases with us. The glorious outcome of the combination of these two conditions is that we become like Him.

The secret for victory is found in trusting Jesus and placing ourselves at His disposal. It is like being a ball in the palm of His hands, cozy and secure. Then He helps us to progress beyond this by throwing us anytime and anywhere at will. Trusting fully in Christ, we are absolutely confident that the hand that holds us is the hand that throws us, and the same hand that guides us and catches us at the end. It does not get better than this, does it? He is indeed the author and finisher of our faith. We choose for the ball to be His by holding it, pitching it, guiding it, and catching it. This is what genuine submission is all about.

Christ's Way to Restoration

3. **Abidance.** This has to do with determination and steadfastness in our walk with Jesus. To highlight the importance of this characteristic of abiding, Jesus mentions it seven times in John 15:4-7. Without abiding in Christ we can do *nothing*. In one verse He says: "I am the vine, you are the branches. He who abides in Me, and I in him, bears much fruit: for without Me you can do nothing" (v. 15). The meaning of this verse became quite clear to me as a child, watching my dad grafting a sapling into a vine. A few weeks later we noticed that one graft was dry and useless. It did not adhere to the parent stock, therefore it could do absolutely nothing. My dad used this as a teaching moment: "In order to be alive and fruitful, we must always be connected with Christ," he said.

This quality of abidance conveys the idea of intimacy and permanency. It is not for a temporary and superficial show, but for a life commitment. The fruitful branch has a living connection with the vine. How does that happen in our daily lives? "Fiber by fiber and vein by vein, become knit with the Vine, and partake of its life . . . As the graft receives life when united to the vine, so the sinner partakes of the divine nature when connected with Christ. Finite mind is united with the infinite God. When thus united, the words of Christ *abide* in us, and we are not actuated by a spasmodic feeling, but a living abiding principle" (*Sons and Daughters of God*, p. 291).

Branches connected with each other must never use this connection as a substitute for abiding in the vine. It is nice to see branches fitting together on a vine, but without them all directly abiding in the vine they become lifeless. Similarly, it is fine for us to have fellowship with the members of Christ's body, but we must first fellowship with Christ. Without directly receiving life and fruitfulness from Him, we can do *nothing* to impart this to others. The two beams forming the shape of the cross illustrate well this priority. The vertical beam is higher and points upward, the horizontal beam is shorter and points sideways. Our priority is to be anchored firmly pointing heavenward to Christ; hence, from that position of strength we view ourselves and others from His perspective.

In other words, as our hearts are lifted upward our hands are stretched outward toward others. John captures this truth when he said, "You may have fellowship with us; and truly our fellowship is with the Father and with His Son Jesus Christ" (1 Jn. 1:3). Ellen White echoes the same idea: "A union of believers with Christ will as a natural result lead to a union with one another, which bond of union is the *most enduring* upon the earth . . . Christians are branches, and only branches, in the living Vine. One branch is not to borrow its sustenance from another. *Our life must come from the parent vine.* It is *only* by personal union with Christ, by communion with Him daily, hourly, that we can bear the fruits of the Holy Spirit . . . Our growth in grace, our joy, our usefulness, all depend on our union with Christ and the degree of faith we exercise in Him" (*Testimonies*, vol. 5, pp. 47, 48;italics supplied).

4. **Perseverance**. This quality has to do with the tenacity to *continue* abiding in Christ. Growth in Christ is a great, but continuation in growth is the ultimate goal. Perseverance must always be linked to abidance. As we abide in Christ, trials and afflictions may descend on us, but perseverance helps us to stay steady and steadfast. We do not hang on to Jesus out of passive resignation, but we enthusiastically embrace Him, persuaded that we will be overcomers in His overcoming. There is a bright light at the end of the tunnel, and victory will be ours if we do not lose heart. We do not persevere because we always feel like it, but because it is the right, wise, and the successful thing to do.

Christ's Way to Restoration

To persevere is not merely to reside in a house for a short while, but to abide for a lifetime. We have had several neighbors who built nice houses only to live in them for a short while, then to sell them and move on. What amazes me is how rootless and transient we have become. I grew up in the biblical culture where there is something permanent about one's home—living in it for many generations. You abide there to keep special memories alive, to preserve family legacy, and to pass on a precious heritage. Doesn't this give us a glimpse of what it means to continue abiding in Jesus?

Perseverance is so indispensable to us even when we are held and sustained in the arms of Jesus. Satan whispers doubt, harasses us with worry, and vexes us with anxiety in order to shake our trust. And if we naively open our hearts to his insinuations, it undermines our trust relationship with our Lord. If we are not awake to Satan's subtleties, he will entice us to fret and worry ourselves away from Christ. To wallow in worry is not necessarily a sin of commission, something deliberate, but rather something we succumb to in our carelessness. The devil is such a subtle deceiver that he does not care what means he uses to lures us away from Christ, as long as he does.

There are three statements of Ellen White that enlighten us about this:

a. "If we *educated* our souls to have more faith, more love, greater patience, a more perfect trust in our heavenly Father, we would have more peace and happiness as we pass through the conflicts of life. The Lord is not pleased to have us *fret* and *worry* ourselves *out of* the arms of Jesus." (*Our High Calling*, p. 120, italics supplied). It is the borrowed anxieties about imagined evils that spoil our daily rest in Jesus. Becoming cumbered with worry, and weighed down with anxiety, shows that we do not totally rely on Him. It is just as possible to *trust* ourselves *into* the arms of Jesus as it is to *fret* ourselves *out* of them. It is so tragic that we frequently fret ourselves out of the arms of Jesus into the waiting arms of Satan.

b. "When brought into trial, we are not to fret and worry. We should *not* rebel, or *worry ourselves out of the hand of Christ.* We are to humble the soul before Christ" (*Signs of the Times*, Feb. 5, 1902; italics supplied). Trials can cause worry, and worry can lead to distrust, and distrust can result in worrying ourselves out of Christ's safety and into the devil's dangerous domain.

c. "If you feel at liberty to moan and groan over bereavements, things that are past, out of your keeping, things that you *cannot change* or alter, you will *neglect the present duties* lying directly in your pathway. Look unto Jesus, who is the Author and Finisher of your faith. Turn your attention from subjects which make you gloomy and sad, for you become an *agent in the hands of the enemy* to multiply gloom and darkness and you will make the atmosphere surrounding your soul dark and forbidding. Although severe afflictions may come upon you, it is *your business* to look up, and see light in Jesus" (*This Day With God*, p. 233; italics supplied).

Here are several factors which mitigate against our continuous abidance in Christ:

- Regretting over things we cannot change.

- Focusing on things that make us gloomy and sad.

- Multiplying a dark atmosphere around us.

Here are the serious consequences of worry, regret, and negativism which fight against our steady walk with our Savior:

- Neglecting today's present opportunities by focusing on regret, gloom, and darkness.

Christ's Way to Restoration

- If such neglect continues, the outcome is dire: becoming agents in the hands of the devil.

It is hard to believe that in taking the wrong course outlined above, we actually change from being agents of Christ to becoming agents of Satan! What is the real remedy for this terrible condition?

- Looking away from self, and from things that make you discouraged and depressed.

- Looking unto Jesus who guards your present and future securely in the palm of His hand.

- Remembering that in the raging storms, Jesus is holding your hand with a grip that will not let go.

5. **Resistance**. In resisting evil with Christ, we need to go not only on the defensive, but on the offensive as well. We must always be ready, united with Christ, to launch preemptive strikes against the enemy. This mode of spiritual resistance implies intentionality and preparedness where things are not left to chance. God's word often admonishes us to be awake, alert, and vigilant in our spiritual warfare against the evil one. Daniel's example illustrates this point. He did not wait for the trial to come his way, he prepared for it ahead of time. "But Daniel *purposed* in his heart that he would defile himself" (Dan. 1:8). Jesus said, "the ruler of this world is coming, and he has *nothing* in Me" (Jn. 14:30).

The demonic forces must be served notice that clad in Christ's formidable armor we are strong and secure. That we are not vulnerable, just waiting haplessly to be attacked by him. The apostle Peter counsels us to humble ourselves before God, be vigilant, and steadfast in the faith as we resist the evil one (1 Pet. 5:8, 9). "Live in contact with the living Christ, and He will hold you firmly by a hand that will never let go. Know and believe the love that God has to us, and you are secure; that love is a fortress impregnable to all the delusions and assaults of Satan. 'The name of the Lord is a strong tower: the righteous runneth into it, and is safe.' Proverbs 18:10" (*Mount of Blessing*, p. 119).

The apostle James gives us three steps to follow in order to resist the devil victoriously. "Therefore submit to God. Resist the devil and he will flee from you" (James 4:7). Here are the progressive steps that must be experienced in this order to assure us of victory:

a. **Submit** ourselves to God, and He will cover us with His righteousness and shield us in His armor. Together with Him we form a formidable front. It is a solid standard that He raises for us against the enemy.

b. **Resist** the devil united with God, and He will prove to be more than a match for him. God does most of the heavy lifting, helping us in our struggle against evil. The implicit trust of king David and king Jehoshaphat in God's power are good examples to mention here. There was absolutely no hope of victory for them without God. David said as he confronted the giant: "This assembly shall know that the Lord does not save with sword and spear; for the battle is the Lord's, and He will give you into our hands" (1 Sam. 7:47). Then in the case of King Jehoshaphat, God told him and the people: "Do not be afraid nor dismayed because of this great multitude, for the battle is not yours but God's . . . You will not need to fight in this battle. Position yourselves, stand still and see the salvation of the Lord who is with you" (2 Chron. 20:15, 17).

They were so submitted to God that their fight was the fight of faith in trusting Him with all their hearts. They did play their part, but it was the part of total reliance on God's power, and trusting obedience in His word. They were so surrounded in God's impregnable shield that the enemy could not penetrate it. For "He who is imbued with the Spirit of Christ abides in Christ. The blow that is aimed at him falls upon the Saviour, who surrounds him with His presence. Whatever comes to him comes from Christ. He has no need to resist evil, for Christ is his defense. Nothing can touch him except by our Lord's permission" (*Mount of Blessing*, p. 71).

c. Satan will **Flee** from us. It is often the case that God's people flee, but it is high time that Satan flees for a change. Our implicit trust and obedience makes the big difference. Satan sees Jesus in us and all around us, and he resigns himself to the stark fact that in fighting us he has to fight Jesus. "We cannot save ourselves from the tempter's powers . . . and when we try to stand in our own strength, we shall become a prey to his devices; but 'the name of the Lord is a strong tower: the righteous runneth into it, and is safe.' Satan trembles and flees at the weakest soul who finds refuge in that mighty name" (*The Desire of Ages*, p. 141).

6. **Genuineness.** We hear the saying that not all that glitters is gold. We are a part of a society that focuses on marketing, appearances, inflated resumes, and giving the right impression. Not only are we awash with plastic products, but our own existence is often plastic and artificial. We are pleasantly surprised when we smell a real flower, handle a genuine wood product, or touch actual stones on a building. It is also serendipitous these days to get acquainted with people who are real, whose heart is genuine, and whose words and deeds are authentic. With such friends, you get what you see, and you see what you get. In their innermost souls they are true to principle. They are truth tellers, for they say what they mean and mean what they say. This is indeed one of the choicest blessings: to become friends with

such persons, for they resemble the authenticity of Christ in their lives.

Christ is the truth and the fountain of it; Satan is the father and fabricator of falsehood. It is not enough to merely give assent to truthful teachings, but to be truthful in the likeness of Christ. He cut through the maze of rationalization and situation ethics by simply saying: "But let your 'Yes' be 'Yes,' and your 'No' be 'No.' For whatever is more than these is from the evil one" (Matt. 5:37). Ellen White echoes what Christ said in cutting through all the excuses and compromises with deception: "Everything that Christians do should be as transparent as the sunlight. Truth is of God; deceptions, *in every one of its myriad forms*, is of Satan; and whoever in any way departs from the straight line of truth is betraying himself into the power of the wicked one" (*Mount of Blessings*, p. 68; italics supplied). We simply cannot presume that we are secure in Jesus while we are deceiving.

The genuine disciples of Christ reflect His character, because He is truth embodied. This is so opposite to what a Christian leader once told me: what matters most is how others perceive you. But outward perception does not always reflect the inner character, hence our focus should not be marketing ourselves but modeling our Savior. The parable of the barren fig tree, Jesus told in Mark 13:6-9, is a case in point. The foliage adorning the tree was admirable and plentiful, giving the outward impression of a healthy and fruitful tree. But when its lustrous leaves were pulled aside, there were no figs to be found.

This barrenness did not result from a lack of care. On the contrary, it received more attention than the other trees. While growing up tending fig trees in our family orchard, I would see the disappointed look on my father's face when he would discover a barren fig tree. He was disappointed because the promising abundant foliage camouflaged the barrenness. Likewise, it is quite a letdown when we see promising young people, with great potential, prove fruitless. All the loving nurture, solid education, and vast opportunities to be Christlike are tragically squandered when they choose their own way instead of Christ's way. It is so sad that today the focus is often on the covering of the fig leaves rather than the covering of Christ's righteousness. The desperate need in our lives, the church, and in society at large is nourishing the fruit of character, not useless pretty leaves.

7. **Righteousness**. This wonderful word with immense implications has not been short on controversy. Is this Christ's righteousness, or is it ours? Is it of an objective nature or subjective? Is it righteousness by faith, works, or both? These are questions people continue on asking. The practical question at hand is, what role does righteousness play in becoming Christlike? How is it a characteristic of Christlikeness? Let us consult the apostle John to help us with these questions:

John in addressing this subject in his first epistle, contrasts truth and deception, with works of light and works of darkness. Consider the false and conflicting claims that John addresses so clearly and practically:

a. If we claim to have fellowship with God *but* walk away from Him into darkness, then "we lie and do not practice the truth" (1 Jn. 1:6).

b. If someone maintains that he knows God *but* does not keep His commandments, then he "is a liar, and the truth is not in him" (2:4).

In Christ's Likeness

c. If a person insists that he is abiding in Christ, then he "ought himself also to walk as He walked" (2:6). To abide in Him *is* to walk with Him. Any other claim is misleading.

d. He who professes that "he is in the light but hates his brother, is in darkness until now" (2:9). The condition of such a one becomes more serious when he continues to confuse light with darkness. He "does not know where he is going, because the darkness has blinded his eyes" (2:11). He becomes so blinded in rationalizing his wrong conduct that he calls darkness light.

e. In this context, blindness may imply deception. That is why John said: "Little children, let no one deceive you." But "deceive you" in what? The clear implication is: claiming righteousness without practicing it. " He who practices righteousness is righteous, just as He is righteous" (1 Jn.3:7). The gnostic philosophers of John's day, indifferent to sin and righteousness, were trying to deceive the believers that they could claim righteousness while devoid of its reality in their lives. Who is righteous then? The one who is, first of all, *born* of God. Consequently, this new birth propels him to live righteously for Christ. "If you know that He is righteous, you know that everyone who practices righteousness is born of Him" (2:29).

f. Those who are careless about sin can in no way be considered righteous. Satan has been indifferent in practicing sin from the beginning; and if we follow his example, we become like him. Indeed, this is the distinguishing mark between those who belong to God and those who belong to Satan: whether they practice righteousness or not. "In this the children of God and the children of the devil are manifested: Whoever does not practice righteousness is not of God" (1 Jn. 3:10). Furthermore, "He who sins is of the devil, for the devil has sinned from the beginning. For this purpose the Son of God was manifested, that He might destroy the works of the devil" (3:8). Again, we need to emphasize this truth: Christ came to save us *from* our sins not *in* our sins. And it is obvious why, because it was sin that got us in trouble in the first place.

There is a such a *vast* difference between *professing* righteousness and *possessing* it. Some enjoy discussing Christ and His righteousness, prayer, and sanctification, yet not much of this is a living reality in their daily experience. Conforming to the world is what is seen, but the transforming into the image of Christ is not. Our hearts may be thrilled with God's promises, but are we willing to live by them? "We build on Christ by obeying His word. It is not he who merely enjoys righteousness, that is righteous, but he who does righteousness. Holiness is not rapture; it is the result of surrendering all to God; it is doing the will of our heavenly Father" (*Mount of Blessing*, p. 149).

Now, let us consider John's positive and practical points about what it means to be righteous, and how that helps us to become more Christlike:

a. God took the initiative to love us first, that while we were yet sinners He sent His Son to be the reconciling Sacrifice (1 Jn. 4:10).

b. This is how God deals with our unrighteousness: He awaits our genuine confession and repentance. "If we confess our sins, He is faithful and just to forgive us our sins and to cleanse us of all unrighteousness" (1 Jn.1:9).

c. The new birth experience is indispensable, and without which we cannot enter the kingdom of God. When we are converted we "practice righteousness" (2:29). Those who are born of God and abide in Him become His children, appropriating their Father's character. Such do not continue to sin (3:9, 6), for as new creatures in Christ they hate sin and love righteousness. When we invite Christ to abide in our hearts, His precious blood "cleanses us from all sin" (1:7).

d. When we are born of God and abide in Him, He replaces our unrighteousness with His righteousness. Therefore, our confessed and buried sins cease to block our communion with Him through prayer. He answers our prayers because "we keep His commandments and do those things that are pleasing in His sight" (3:22).

e. When we abide in Christ and do His will, we continue abiding with Him *forever* (2:17).

f. By God's empowering grace, we become overcomers of evil, "because He who is in you is greater than he who is in the world" (Jn. 4:4). Moreover, "For whatever is born of God overcomes the world. And this is the victory that has overcome the world–our faith" in the Son of God (1 Jn. 5:4, 5).

g. God's love is defined as keeping His commandments which are not burdensome (5:3). Such genuine and responsible love liberates us from anxiety and fear. "There is no fear in love; but perfect love casts out fear" (4:18).

h. When the Lord frees us to genuinely love as He loves, then we become *loyal* to Him and our brothers and sisters in Him. This love and loyalty moved Christ to love us to the end, and that should move us to do likewise to them. There is so much betrayal and disloyalty among so-called Christians, and it behooves us, especially in these last days, to manifest unswerving loyalty. Hopefully, this can help us to compensate for all the unfortunate disloyalty that occurs all too often.

i. Our continuous abidance in Christ and obedience to Him not only casts out fear, but gives us confidence to meet Him when He comes again. We become so comfortable walking with Him here, so accustomed to His company, that it prepares us to continue this enduring fellowship in heaven. "And now, little children, abide in Him, that when He appears, we may have confidence and not be ashamed before Him at His coming" (1 Jn. 2:28). "The more the heart is wrapped up in Christ, the more secure is the treasure in the eternal world" (*Reflecting Christ*, p. 287).

j. The ultimate outcome of becoming more Christlike in this world is that we shall be like Him when He returns. We become pure in Christ's purity as we joyously await His blessed appearing. John looks forward to the future at His appearing when he writes that "when He is revealed, we shall be like Him, for we shall see Him as He is" (3:2).

The ancient book of Zechariah encapsulates the completeness of the full gospel. In chapter three he outlines the three progressive steps of becoming righteous and Christlike. I refer to Zechariah's dynamic steps as: from guilt to glory.

a. The *Covering* in Christ's rich robe of righteousness replaces our filthy garments (Zech. 3:4-6). This is what we refer to as justification by faith in Christ.

b. The *Walking* with Jesus here in this world until He comes. "If you will walk in My ways, and if you will keep My command . . ." (3:7a). This is sanctification by faith in Christ, best described as *walking* with Jesus as Enoch walked.

c. The *Walking* with Christ there in heaven when He comes again. "I will give you places to walk among these who stand here" (3:7b). This is what glorification by faith in Christ is about. Walking with Christ here in this world leads us to walk with Him there in heaven. Enoch's continual walk with Christ here evolved into his walk with Christ in glory.

8. **Advancement** in sanctification, which is not merely a goal but a way of life. There is not a stopping place where we

can rest on our laurels and feel we have arrived. Even in glory we will ever continue to advance in our knowledge of God. True sanctification is the persistent pursuit of spiritual excellence with steady advancement. This is how the Holy Spirit fashions us to be more Christlike, but this process can be arduous. For example, it takes breaking, chiseling, polishing, and refining to produce a precious diamond. Such arduous work will help us to be "molded after the model of Christ's character. His own image is to be reflected in the polished character of His human agent, and the stone is to be fitted for the heavenly building" (*Son and Daughters of God*, p. 319).

The apostle Paul, with all his spiritual advancement, constantly felt the need to keep on advancing. Not in order to be saved, but because he was saved by God's grace. Christ's salvation was so overwhelming and empowering that in gratitude Paul would have sacrificed all for it. Humbly he testified: "Not that I have already attained, or am already perfected; but I press on . . . Brethren, I do not count myself to have apprehended; but one thing I do, forgetting those things which are behind and reaching forward to those things which are ahead. I press toward the goal for the prize of the upward call of God in Christ Jesus" (Phil. 3:12-14).

Paul was martyred under the blade of a sword, ever doing his utmost best for his precious Savior and Lord. Through it all he was more than a conqueror with Jesus. Through stonings and storms, buffetings and beatings, perplexities and persecutions, the Lord polished him into a precious stone for His holy temple. May our hearts be greatly moved as we read his inspiring last will and testament: "But I am already being poured out as a drink offering, and the time of my departure is at hand. I have fought the good fight, I have finished the race, I have kept the faith" (2 Tim. 4:6, 7). He loved Christ's appearing as he wore

His crown of suffering. Now he was waiting for His glorious crown of righteousness.

The justification by faith that he preached was confirmed by the Spirit's sanctification in his life, to be culminated in the glorification Christ was to grant him at His appearing. This inspired insight about holiness is what aptly describes Paul's experience, and by God's grace should describe ours. "Holiness is not rapture: it is an entire surrender of the will to God; it is living by every word that proceeds from the mouth of God; it is doing the will of our heavenly Father; it is trusting God in trial, in darkness as well as in the light; it is walking by faith and not by sight; it is relying on God with unquestioning confidence, and resting in His love" (*Acts of the Apostles*, p. 51).

9. **Persecution.** Many Christians in our culture think that following Christ is embarking on a path covered with roses. With the prosperity theology that is being preached today, one would think being poor is sinful and becoming rich is righteousness embodied. The priority question for such is, what can Christ and the church do to help me have fun and be happy? Christ's ideals of self-denial, submission, dying to self are not in vogue. The persecuted Paul reminds us that "all who desire to live godly in Christ Jesus will suffer persecution" (2 Tim. 3:12). Notice how inclusive persecution is: *all* who are godly in Christ will suffer it in one way or the other, making no exception for any. If persecution does not befall us, it may indicate that the devil is not worried about us, and does not want to rattle our cage. But if persecution for righteousness' sake is inflicted upon us, then Satan is worried and angry that we may escape his bondage. You see, there will be no glorious crown in heaven for us to wear, unless we carry our cross here. Carrying the cross of persecution with patient endurance is not something to shield ourselves from. The unbiblical theory of pre-tribulationism, that

In Christ's Likeness

most Christians adhere to, teaches that Christ will secretively come before the time of persecution to rapture the believers from it. The Bible clearly teaches that persecution is an integral part of being a committed believer. It is true that the offense of the cross has not ceased.

Jesus Himself experienced persecution more than anyone else. Even as a youngster still living at home, Jesus suffered persecution at the hands of His own siblings. Their enmity against His gospel "was most painful to Him in His home . . . instead of comforting Him, their spirit and words only wounded His heart. His sensitive nature was tortured, His motives misunderstood, His work uncomprehended" (*The Desire of ages*, p. 326). Furthermore, He did not look forward to go home because of their persecution. "These things made His path a thorny one to travel. So pained was Christ by the misapprehension in His own home that it was a relief to Him to go where it did not exist" (*Ibid.*).

Persecution is provoked when we are Christlike in our conduct before those of the world. Indeed, the more we reflect Christ's character, the more the opposition intensifies. Because Christ in His daily life "would give no license for the exercise of the evil passions of our nature, He aroused the fiercest opposition and enmity. So it will be with all who will live godly in Christ Jesus. Between righteousness and sin, love and hatred, truth and falsehood, there is an irrepressible conflict. When one presents the love of Christ and the beauty of holiness, he is drawing away the subjects of Satan's kingdom, and the prince of evil is aroused. Persecution and reproach await all who are imbued with the Spirit of Christ" (*Mount of Blessing*, p. 29).

Christlike believers do not have a persecution complex, desiring to bring it on prematurely; but they are prepared to suf-

Christ's Way to Restoration

fer for Christ's cause. "Blessed are those who are persecuted for righteousness' sake," Christ said in His beatitude, "for theirs is the kingdom of heaven" (Matt. 5:10). Here Christ pronounces happiness not sadness upon those who are persecuted. It is of the highest honor to share in Christ's suffering. Real joy springs forth from a persecuted heart as in the case of Paul and Silas in the Philippian dungeon. Their exuberance in song and praise surprised all except them, for they were sure that they were united as one in Christ's suffering. "Those who love their Redeemer will rejoice at every opportunity of sharing with Him humiliation and reproach. The love they bear their Lord makes suffering for His sake sweet . . . Being partakers of Christ's sufferings, they are destined to be partakers of His glory" (*Mount of Blessing*, pp. 31, 32).

Revilement is a close cousin to persecution, but it is more focused against one's reputation and character. To be stigmatized by slander can cause more suffering than to be stricken with stones. It is human to be protective of our reputation in defense of our character. But we need to make a distinction between reputation and character. Reputation is what people think of us, but character is how God views us. It is unfortunate that we sometimes pay more attention to what people think of us rather than what God thinks of us. We stand ready to valiantly defend our reputation much more than building our character. But what ultimately matters is where we stand with God. Revilers may sully our reputation, but cannot change our character.

Was the pure and perfect Redeemer reviled? Of course. Did that in any way undermine His character? Never. We are truly honored and blessed when we join our Lord in being maligned for the sake of the truth. "Blessed are you when they revile and persecute you, and say all kinds of evil against you falsely for My

160

sake," He encourages us, His present-day disciples. "Rejoice and be exceedingly glad, for great is your reward in heaven" (Matt. 5:11, 12). We are not to be sad but "exceedingly glad" and honored to join the reviled prophets before us, awaiting with them our glorious reward in heaven.

Here is more about the revilement of Christ's reputation, and how that may encourage us when we are reviled. "There was never one who walked among men more cruelly slandered than the Son of man. He was derided and mocked because of His unswerving obedience to the principles of God's holy law. They hated Him without a cause" (*Mount of Blessing*, p. 32). Do you see how differently we need to view reputation and character? "While slander may blacken the reputation, it cannot stain the character. That is in God's keeping." When revilers "blacken" our reputation, they are dealing with the exterior only, like stirring up dust. Like dust, slander cannot "stain," or be absorbed into the interior of our Christlike character. A devoted disciple's "words, his motives, his actions, may be misrepresented and falsified, but he does not mind it, because he has greater interest at stake" (*Ibid.*).

Let us look beyond the visible to God's invisible, beyond what is passing to what is everlasting. Our reward is the glories of heaven, to be enjoyed with the Redeemer and the redeemed for ever! In the meantime, let us keep in mind Christ's encouragement. "Christ is acquainted with all that is misunderstood and misrepresented by men. His children can afford to wait in calm patience and trust, no matter how much maligned and despised" (*Ibid.*). We are embraced by Christ our defense, accepted in the Him the Beloved, and sheltered under His protective wings. "The Father's presence encircled Christ, and nothing befell Him but that which infinite love permitted for the blessing of the world. Here was His source of comfort, and it is for us. He who is imbued with the Spirit of Christ abides in Christ. The blow that is aimed at him falls upon the Saviour, who surrounds him with His presence. Whatever comes to Him comes from Christ" (*Ibid.*, p. 71).

10. **Consecration.** This characteristic assures us of doing things Christ's way in our holy quest of becoming like Him. To "consecrate" is to set someone or something apart for sacred or holy use. It is to devote or dedicate one's self or gifts entirely to God's service. The sacred act of consecration brings to mind the messages found in two Bible texts and two hymns. The first text: Christ "has loved us and given Himself for us, an offering and a sacrifice to God for a sweet smelling aroma" (Eph. 5:2). The second one: Paul beseeches us to "present your bodies a living sacrifice, holy, acceptable to God, which is your reasonable service" (Rom. 12:1). He first offered Himself as a living and holy Sacrifice, and we respond by offering ourselves as living and holy sacrifices. Here is the first hymn of life consecration:

"Take my life, and let it be consecrated, Lord, to Thee;

Take my hands, and let them move at the impulse of Thy love,

Take my will and make it Thine; it shall be no longer mine;

Take my heart, it is Thine own! It shall be Thy royal throne."

Jesus revealed in His holy life the ultimate expression in consecration: sacrificing His life to redeem fallen humanity. And when we consecrate our lives to Him and His service, we are in essence responding to His consecration to us. Certainly our entire consecration to Christ is what it takes to become Christlike.

In Christ's Likeness

This is what it means to consecrate our bodies as a living and holy sacrifice to Christ and others. The members of our bodies become totally dedicated to His service: our life, our hands, our feet, our voice, our lips, our silver and gold, our will, our heart, our love, and our self. Christ gave to us His sacred body on the cross: His heart, His hands, His feet, His eyes, His voice, and His love. We are the members of the body of Christ. All the members of His body are given in His great Sacrifice for us. Here is the other hymn of consecration:

"We are His hands to touch the world around us. We are His feet to go where He may lead.

We are His eyes to see the need in others. We are His voice to tell of His return, and

We are His love burning in the darkness. We are His love shining in the night."

Just think of it: On the cross Jesus gave us His broken heart, hence we are His heart for a broken humanity. We are His heart that resonates with sympathy. He gave us His nail-scarred hands, hence we are His hands to reach out in helping others. He gave us His torn feet, hence we are His feet to walk His love in the paths He leads. He gave us His eyes when He closed them shut, hence we are His eyes to look with a heart that throbs with compassion. He gave us His parched lips as He spoke His last words, hence we are His voice to speak hope and affirmation.

To think of it this way, as the body of Christ, is so enabling in becoming Christlike. What would Jesus do with the members of His body that He gave to us on the cross? For example, let us ask ourselves these questions about our daily lives: We are His hands, so what would His hands touch? We are His feet, so where would His feet go? We are His eyes, so what would His eyes look at? We are His lips, so what words would His lips

Christ's Way to Restoration

speak? Thus by God's grace, we do what Christ does, and shun what He does not do. We have Christ's mind and His heart to control and nourish our entire being. Thus in total submission to His will, and as consecrated living members of His body, we are becoming more and more like Him until we see Him face to face in glory.

Earnest and Urgent Appeal

I earnestly and urgently appeal to you and me that we must, by God's grace, become Christlike before it is too late. Time is fast approaching for Christ to come, and *now* is the acceptable time. There is absolutely no time to waste, and it should not be for us business as usual, for these are unusual times we live in. It is not enough to be informed about Him, but by beholding Him to be transformed into His likeness, for without this we will not be able to see God. He spares no effort in preparing us to be loving and loyal citizens of His kingdom.

Please let us contemplate in our hearts and apply in our lives this inspired and compelling counsel: Jesus "waits with unwearied love to hear the confessions of the wayward and to accept their penitence. He watches for some return of gratitude from us, as the mother watches for the smile of recognition from her beloved child. He would have us understand how earnestly and tenderly His heart yearns over us. He invites us to take our trials to His sympathy, our sorrows to His love, our wounds to His healing, our weakness to His strength, our emptiness to His fullness. Never has one been disappointed who came unto Him . . . As we make Christ our daily companion we shall feel that the powers of an unseen world are all around us; and by looking unto Jesus we shall become assimilated to His image. By beholding we become changed" (*Mount of Blessing*, p. 84, 85).

Discussion Questions

1. How can we share in the testimony of John the Baptist that Christ must increase and we must decrease? What is "sticking out of us" for the world to see? Is it self or is it the Savior?

2. "A Christian is the highest type of man, a representative of Christ" (*Evangelism*, p. 641). Compare this definition with yours of what a genuine Christian is like. How do we become Christlike?

3. Plenty of costly research has been done on the effects of the media on the human mind. Some doubt its detrimental effects. How does this fallacy contrast with: by beholding we become changed?

4. We have all watched athletes compete in the Olympics. We have been impressed by how willing they were to adopt or abandon anything that would enhance their chances to win. What are some practices that we need to adopt or abandon to guarantee our victory with Jesus?

5. What is the highest position in life? What is the greatest recognition? How does one flow out of the other? We often focus on climbing the ladder but not on carrying the cross. What do you think?

6. What are the three consecutive steps for spiritual victory outlined in James 4:7? Why is it essential to follow these steps in order? What happens when we do not submit to Christ first?

7. A genuine Christian is one who does not merely *profess* Christ with his *mouth*, but does *possess* Him in his *heart*. How can Christ take full possession of our hearts? Advancement in sanctification is more than a goal, it is a way of life. How is this so?

Christ's Way to Restoration

8. The gnostic philosophers of John's day taught that one can claim righteousness while devoid of its reality. Do we witness such misleading teachings in our day? If yes, in what forms?

9. What is the most cruel form of persecution for righteousness' sake? Which is harder: to be struck with stones or to be stigmatized by slander? Explain why. What is the difference between character and reputation?

10. What do you think of these ideas? Christ gave His body on the cross as a living sacrifice for each one of us. In receiving this gift, we become members of His body. Therefore, we become His heart, His hands, His feet, His voice to others around us. How would this awesome realization help us to become more Christlike?

In Christ's Likeness

CHAPTER SEVEN

Why Not Choose Life

Bobby had been committed to God, and active in the youth program at the church he attended with his godly parents. Things seemed to be going quite well spiritually, and the future looked promising in his plan to become a minister. In his junior year of high school, he met a pretty girl with whom he soon became infatuated. She differed from him in principles and values, yet her charm and flirtation won him over. To please her, he began to compromise the principles His parents had imparted to him from childhood. In stealing his heart, she also stole his virtue, his devotion to Christ, and his commitment to ministry. She became his bewitching idol, sacrificing his godly ideals at her altar.

After a few weeks of this downward spiritual spiral, I felt impressed to visit him in his home and see if I could help in some way. He was gracious to see me, but adamant about the course he was taking. His life was his business, and he was choosing to live it the way he wanted. He was so blinded to any reasonable counsel I suggested, as if he were in a different world. He could not see beyond the confines of the cage he was trapped in. He seemed to be willing to sacrifice anything or anyone at the shrine of his romantic sentiments. I encouraged him to reconsider his rebellious course from God and biblical principles. I also appealed to him to honor his loving and godly parents, and the moral values they had instilled in him.

He abruptly dismissed everything I said by saying that his free choice to do whatever he pleased was his own business. Someone had taught him that God was pleased and honored with any decision he would make–right or wrong–as long as he exercised his freedom of choice. The more he talked about his newly acquired idea, the more I sensed that he viewed free choice as a demigod to be worshiped. That the emphasis was on making a decision, but not on making the right decision. Listen with me to his convoluted thinking: nothing is wrong with making a wrong choice, he rationalized, as long as you make it; even if it is a choice against God's word. For God is so unconditionally loving and accepting regardless of anyone's disobedience, that He will always be near, and will always bring us back to Him at some point in the future. In the meantime, he wanted to have fun living recklessly, presuming that God would work everything out for the good.

The Conditional God

Tragically, he and his girlfriend were killed in an automobile accident the following night while drinking and driving. How utterly sad and tragic! Not all those who rebel against God come back. And God is not always near, and cannot always be found. His responsible love never allows Him to take a neutral stance when it comes to our decision making. He cares enough to warn us to seek Him now at this acceptable time, and compassionately He pleads with us to return from our wayward ways. Listen to what He says in Isaiah 55:6, 7. "Seek the Lord while He may be found, call upon Him while He is near. Let the wicked forsake his way, and the unrighteous man his thoughts; let him return to the Lord, and He will have mercy on him; and to our God, for He will abundantly pardon."

Here are three significant points from God's urgent entreaty through Isaiah: First, He pleads with us to seek Him *while* He may be found, and *while* He is near, clearly implying that He may not always be found or be near. Let us choose *now* to seek and find Him *while* we have the opportunity, and to enter into His presence *while* the door of mercy is still open. Second, this chance is greatly jeopardized by clinging to our stubborn rebellion. But this need not be if we repent and separate ourselves from our sinful ways. Third, on the condition that we earnestly heed His counsel, He will pardon and restore us to His favor.

I discussed the above text from Isaiah in one of the churches I spoke at, and I was surprised that a good number of the members did not agree with the conditionality of God's plea. They bypassed the clearly implied conditionality of the text, insisting that God would always be found and would always be near no matter what. They insisted that it mattered little if they persisted in their rebellion, or if they held on to their sinful ways, that He would always be close. That was because of His unconditional love for them. They seemed to be so blindly steeped in this unbalanced idea of God's unconditional love and acceptance in dealing with people. It did not matter to God how deliberately they persisted in their rebellious ways, that He would always be there for them. While they doggedly persisted in their relentless rebellion, He would always be present in their lives.

What an irresponsible, presumptuous, and extreme way of thinking! Let the prophet Isaiah say more about this crucial issue. In the first chapter of his book, he actually presents God as conditional in the ways He deals with us. Look at how God is repulsed by His people's false religious practices, while pleading with them to repent of their evil ways. "I cannot endure your iniquity and the sacred meeting. Your New Moons and your appointed feasts My soul hates," God laments. "When you spread out your hands, I will hide My eyes from you; even though you make many prayers, I will not hear. Your hands are full of blood" (Isa. 1:13-15).

Isaiah is so balanced in presenting God's approach to His people. He says that God is near us on the *condition* of contriteness and humbleness. "I dwell in the high and holy place, with him who has a contrite and humble spirit, and to revive the spirit of the humble, and to revive the heart of the contrite ones" (57:15). He desires to be near them in order to save them, but there is a problem: their choice to continue in their sin blocks Him from accomplishing that. "But your iniquities have separated you from God; and your sins have hidden His face from you, so that He will not hear" (59:1, 2). Notice that God's reaction of closing His eyes and deafening His ears was not what He really desired, but it was their sustained sinning that brought this about.

Warning and Hope

When God gives His warnings He always offers hope, a way of escape if we so choose to walk in it. "Come now, and let us reason together," He calls on us. "Though your sins are like scarlet, they shall be as white as snow." Then right after His ardent appeal, He commences with His conditional "if." According to God, there are conditions to meet for His promises to be realized: "If you are willing and obedient, you shall eat the good of the land; but if you refuse and rebel, you shall be devoured by

171

the sword" (Isa. 1:19, 20). Earlier in verses 16 and 17, He urges His wayward people to "Cease to do evil, learn to do good."

God's great love is so evident in the book of Hosea, for He pleads with and pursues the sinner to the very end. But even there we see His conditionality in dealing with the people He loves so much. This is how He pleads with them when they persist in their idolatry. "With their flocks and herds they shall go to seek the Lord, but they will not find Him; He has withdrawn Himself from them" (Hos. 5: 6). This text in Hosea is precisely the answer to the conditionality in Isaiah 55:6 that should clarify any ambiguity about its meaning. "Seek the Lord while He may found." The word "while" implies that He may not always be found. Hosea is quite clear: when they *sought* the Lord, they *could not find* Him. Why? Because He actually *had withdrawn* Himself from them.

The wise Solomon is quite clear about the presumptuous fallacy that God is always there regardless of our deliberate defiance of Him. God through wisdom says: "Then they will call on me, but I will not answer; they will seek me diligently, but they will not find me" (Prov. 1:28). It is obvious here that sometimes God *does not answer*, and is *not to be found*. But why is that? "Because they hated knowledge and did not choose the fear of the Lord, they would have none of my counsel and despised all my reproof" (Prov. 1:29, 30). Even though God allows us the freedom to make even a wrong decision, yet He is never neutral, He pleads with us to choose right. "However, men are free moral agents, and God does not prevent the results of a course of their own choosing. At the same time *He does all He can to prevent* men from making a contrary choice." (*The SDA Bible Commentary*, vol. 3, p. 951; italics supplied).

Why Not Choose Life

The misconception about a neutral and unconditional God is so misleading and dangerous, because it hides behind a religious facade, and encourages blind and risky presumption. One can hardly escape the conditional factor in many biblical narratives, promises, and warnings. "The Bible is full of conditions" (*Selected Messages*, bk. 1, p. 378). Also it "should be remembered that the promises and threatenings of God are alike conditional" (*Ibid.*, p. 67). By God's grace we are to desist now from doing evil and move toward doing good. Contrary to popular and easy religion, the Bible religion urges us to be intentional and deliberate in trusting and obeying God, and in shunning distrust and disobedience to Him.

Conditionality and Neutrality

While Ellen White clearly believes in the message of salvation by faith in Christ, she does not mince words about the human intentionality and cooperation in this process. Let us balance the first part of her next statement with the second part in order to understand this divine/human cooperation. "When it is in the heart to obey God, when efforts are put forth to this end, Jesus accepts this disposition and effort as *man's best service*, and He *makes up* for the *deficiency* with His own *divine merit.*" Now the second part: "But He will *not* accept those who *claim* to have faith in Him, and yet are *disloyal* to His commandments. We hear a great deal about *faith*, but we need to hear a *great deal more* about *works*. Many are *deceiving* their own souls by living an *easy-going, accommodating, crossless* religion. But Jesus says, 'If any man comes after Me, let him deny himself, and take up his cross, and follow Me" (*Ibid.*, 382). "The desire for an easy religion that requires no striving, no self-denial, no divorce from the follies of the world, has made the doctrine of faith, and faith only, a popular doctrine" (*The Great Controversy*, p. 472).

Christ's Way to Restoration

No other author in recent history spoke more eloquently and appreciatively about the greatness of God's love than Ellen White. But in the above statement she tries to bring about balance in emphasizing God's love, but not to the detriment of the essential human response. "The religion which makes of *sin a light matter*, *dwelling* upon the *love of God* to the sinner *regardless of his actions*, only *encourages* the sinner to believe that God will *receive him* while he *continues* in that which he *knows to be sin*. This is what some are doing who profess to believe present truth. The truth is kept *apart* from the life, and that is the reason it has *no power* to convict and convert the soul" (*Testimonies*, vol. 5, p. 540; italics supplied).

What is the problem here? Where is the imbalance? While overemphasizing one aspect we necessarily de-emphasize the other aspect. Let's look carefully at several components of this imbalance in the above statement. One, sinful behavior is treated lightly or with indifference. Two, God's love of the sinner is dwelt upon, but no attention is paid to the sin itself. The sinner's sinful actions are no big deal to them. What are the serious consequences of such imbalance? One, it encourages the sinner to presume on God's love. Two, he deceives himself that he does not have to repent, for God will receive and support him anyway. Three, he becomes emboldened by the misplaced sympathy and support of others to persist in his deliberate sinful behavior. Four, the dichotomy continues in divorcing the right concepts from real life. Five, consequently, he becomes devoid of God's transforming power to impact people's lives.

"We must not, as a people, become careless and look upon sin with indifference. The camp needs purging. All who name the name of Christ need to watch and pray and guard the avenues of the soul; for Satan is at work to corrupt and destroy if the least advantage is given him . . . Sin is among us, and it is not seen to be exceedingly sinful . . . Walking in the light, running in the way of God's commandments, does not give the idea that we can stand still and do nothing. We must be advancing" (*Testimonies*, vol. 3, p. 476).

The balanced and exhortative message of the prophet Amos is intentional and conditional: "Seek good and not evil, that you may live; so the Lord God of hosts will be with you . . . Hate evil, love good; establish justice in the gate. It may be that the Lord of hosts will be gracious to the remnants of Joseph" (Amos 5:14, 15). God's desired spiritual outcome for us in His graciousness is His presence with us, and His gift of abundant life. But there are conditions right in the midst of these blessings: First, seek and love good. Second, shun evil and hate it. Third, establish justice in the gate. *If these conditions are met*, then His grace, presence, and life become ours. But by the implied sense, the reverse is true: *if such conditions are not complied with*, then grace, presence, and life cease to be ours.

It may come as a surprise to some of us the way we normally view one of the most cherished promises of the Bible. "For God so loved the world that He gave His only begotten son" (Jn. 3:16). We focus on the first part about God's great love, as we should, but we bypass the second part which is conditional, "that whoever believes in Him should not perish but have everlasting life." The use of "whoever believes in Him" here implies that *some would choose to believe, some would not*. Then the use of "should not perish" implies *desire and possibility*. In other words, if we choose not to believe we would perish and not have everlasting life. For us not to perish requires us to meet the conditions of trust, submission, and abidance in Christ.

John in his first epistle resonates with what he said in his gospel. Everlasting life is found in the Son, and if we want eternal life we must meet the *condition* of having the Son live in our hearts. "And this is the testimony: that God has given us eternal life, and this life is in His Son. He who has the Son has life; he who does not have the Son of God does not have life" (1 Jn. 5:11, 12). The gift of God's Son is a most costly gift, but it is a free gift for us. The only way to appreciate this precious gift is to accept it and appropriate it by faith in our lives.

A balanced approach brings about equilibrium to our spiritual life. Such is anchored in the truth of God's unchangeable word, and is experienced in His practical life principles. Choices and decisions are serious matters not to be trifled with, for they determine the course of our life and destiny. Let us not be, or encourage others to be, so impatient that we make hasty but irrevocable decisions. Whenever we are faced with making a determinative decision, let us decide not for the sake of deciding, but decide for the right reasons. Life is fashioned by life decisions. The words of the old hymn ring so true: "Once to every man and nation comes the moment to decide, in the strife of truth and falsehood, for the good or evil side . . . And the choice goes on forever 'twixt that darkness and the light."

Contending Forces at Work

There is a raging battle being waged for the control of our minds, a fierce conflict contending for our very souls and destinies. The battlefield is our heart, for out of its choices proceed the issues of life. There is no appeasement or neutrality between the forces of good and the forces of evil. These contending forces are in the unmitigated business of winning us over. But no matter how fierce the contention between these opposing forces, we still have the power to choose. Daily choices, daily decisions—this is the stuff that determines our destinies, forever.

Why Not Choose Life

We are so fortunate that Christ is our victorious General in this decisive battle. He has already won the victory for us on the cross. The crucial question for us is this: will we accept and appropriate this victory in our daily lives by choosing to be on Christ's winning side? We have nothing to lose but our fetters, but everything to gain, even eternal life. "You *cannot* have faith that the Lord will keep you by His loving kindness, and by His truth continually preserve you, when you do not *place yourselves* in the channel of light. Then shun bad companions, and *choose* the good" (*Sons and Daughters of God*, p. 317; italics supplied).

Daniel, in spite of all evil enticements, was purposeful against defilement and impurity. He had all the freedom of choice to dishonor God in a heathen land, but he chose what was right. David, a man after God's own heart, chose to follow God's way. How did he do that? He said: "I have chosen the way of truth; Your judgments I have laid before me. I cling to your testimonies; O Lord, do not put me to shame! I will run in the way of Your commandments, for You shall enlarge my heart. Teach me, O Lord, the way of Your statutes, and I shall keep it to the end" (Ps. 119:30-33).

Let us follow *David's progress in deciding* with all his heart to be after God's own heart. First, he *chose* to walk in the way of truth. Second, he focused on God by choosing to set His judgments as his priority. Third, he chose to cling or cleave to His testimonies. In other words, David decided to embrace God's will. Fourth, he intentionally decided to run in God's way. Walking with God led him to run with Him, which implies progress in their relationship. Thus by this spiritual advance, his heart would be enlarged to appropriate more of the divine character in his life. Fifth, David's profound relationship with God is directly linked to his choice, his walk, his focus, his union, and his run as he advanced forward.

Christ's Way to Restoration

How did David experience all of this? How did he go about this spiritual progress in his life? He was intentional and decisive. He loved and followed God with his whole heart, he longed to be with Him, he delighted in devoting himself to His way, and he was quick to trust and obey Him (Ps. 119:34-60). David was greatly concerned about the people's double-mindedness and rebellious attitude against God's ways, and wanted to urge them to repent and obey His law before it was too late. "Did the contempt shown to the law of God extinguish David's loyalty? Hear his words. He calls upon God to interfere and vindicate His honor, to show that there is a God, that there are *limits to His forbearance*, that it is possible to so *presume* upon the mercy of God as to *exhaust* it" (Manuscript 27, 1899; italics supplied).

King Saul, David's predecessor, preferred placating God with a sacrifice rather than simply obeying Him. He wanted the power of his selfish will to prevail, rather than the greater power of his obedience. He ended up choosing wilful disobedience, thus cutting himself off from the source of his power and salvation. "There is *no safety* except in strict obedience to the word of God. All His promises are made upon *condition* of faith and obedience, and a failure to comply with His commandments *cut off* the fulfillment to us of the rich provisions of the Scriptures. We should not follow *impulse*, nor rely on the *judgment of men*; we should look to the *revealed will* of God and walk according to His definite commandment, no matter what circumstances may surround us . . . Saul was in disfavor with God, and yet unwilling to humble his heart in penitence. What he lacked in real piety he would try to make up by his zeal in the forms of religion" (*Patriarchs and Prophets*, pp. 621, 622).

Why Not Choose Life

Decide for the Right

We heard from Daniel, the great prophet of the exile; from David, the greatest king of Israel; and from Solomon, the wisest king of his time. We heard from them as to what it means to choose to love and serve God. Now let us hear from Moses, whose face shone with the glory of God. The words of his final will and testament (Deut. 30:14-20) took the form of a challenge to urge his people to make the right decisions. So compelling but practical were his words. "But the word [God's] is very near you, in your mouth and in your heart, that you may do it" (30:14). God's holy word is His perfect revealed will, and the foundation of our experience and character. He does not coerce us to adopt it, but He counsels us to consent and cooperate with Him to live it. It is right here near to us, professed from our mouth, possessed in our heart, and applied in our lives.

Then Moses challenges the people to choose, but to choose right. They were totally free to choose evil, cursing, and death, but He urges them to be wise and choose good, blessing, and life. "See, I have set before you today life and good, death and evil" (30:15). God not only urges them to make the right choice, but He commands them to do it, while maintaining their freedom of choice. He said: "I command you today to love the Lord your God, to walk in His ways, and to keep His commandments" in order that you may live and be blessed (3:16). Here is the condition: if we want God to bless us and give us an abundant life, then we must decide to love Him wholeheartedly, which leads us to follow and obey Him.

But the condition on the other hand is that if the heart is not with God, then evil and death will befall them. "But if your heart turns away so that you do not hear, and are drawn away, and worship other gods and serve them," He warns, "I announce to you today that you shall surely perish; you shall not prolong your days in the land you cross over the Jordan to go in and possess" (30:17, 18).

After God clearly sets forth before them the conditions for life and death, He concludes by making a most solemn and urgent appeal to choose life and blessings. He calls upon the entire inhabitants of heaven and earth to serve as witnesses. There is absolutely no hint of coercion in God's appeal, but there is abundant evidence therein as to where He stands. His impassioned plea, full of powerful persuasion, leaves no doubt whatsoever that He wants them to make the right choice. Listen to His fervent appeal: "I call heaven and earth as witnesses today against you, that I have set before you life and death, blessing and cursing; therefore choose life, that both you and your descendants may live" (30:19).

Notice how He encourages them to *make a decision*, not for the sake of merely making a decision and getting it over with, but for making the *right decision*. May this serve as a caution to us as we counsel others, wavering in the valley of decision, to exercise wisely their freedom of choice. Our God-given priority in this weighty matter is not to press people for a decision regardless of consequences, but to persuade them to make the *right decision* based on God's sure word. This is God's approach that we ought not to veer away from. He makes His appeal in a winsome way, promising rich rewards. In freely choosing blessings and life, "you may love the Lord your God, that you may obey His voice, and that you may cling to Him, for He is your life and the length of your days" (30:20). Loving the Lord naturally leads to obeying Him, which leads to clinging to Him, and to receiving His life.

Why Not Choose Life

Haughty Hearts and Itching Ears

The Lord well knows the deceitfulness and rationalization of the human heart that insists on going its wrong way. He addresses those rebellious souls who defiantly bless themselves in response to His curse against them. Their rebellious reaction is: if God does not bless us, then we will bless ourselves. We can go ahead and bless ourselves, managing fine without His blessing. Moses calls this defiant attitude a "root of bitterness" that if one "hears the words of this curse, he blesses himself in his heart, saying, 'I shall have peace, even though I follow the dictates of my heart' as though the drunkard can be included with the sober. The Lord would not spare him . . ." (Deut. 29:18-20).

Rebellious persons, like the one described by Moses, turn things upside down in calling drunkenness soberness. They become so arrogant that they bless themselves knowing they are cursed. They claim to have peace while devoid of peace, slavishly following the wilfulness of their own hearts. Self becomes their slave master to serve and to worship. Therefore, to them the end justifies the means. They become so bewitched by their own folly that they twist God's truth, alter it, recast it, manipulate it, and even reject it if it does not fit their self-serving schemes. But they do not stop here, but go even further in their precipitous fall from grace. They strive to seduce others to join them in their rebellion, flagrantly flaunting their folly as wisdom everywhere.

Those who thus deny or rationalize their rebellious choices by blessing themselves, become so self-absorbed, prideful, and unreasonable. They are the kind of persons the apostle Paul warns Timothy about: "For the time will come when they will not endure sound doctrine, but according to their own desires, because they have itching ears, they will heap up for themselves teachers; and they will turn their ears away from the truth, and be turned aside to fables" (2 Tim. 4:3, 4). Paul, just before he was martyred, was preparing Timothy for such a time of defiant disregard of God's word. He was to be ready to uplift the truth, though it may have been challenging or inconvenient.

With love and patience, Timothy was to convict, censure, exhort, and encourage the wayward to trust and obey God's truth. Paul was preparing Timothy for what some would rashly do after his imminent departure:

1. They would *not endure* sound biblical teaching. This would bother them so much that they could not stand it. They would close their ears and seal their hearts against it, because it would contradict their own selfish desires.

2. They would have *itching ears* to bend the Scripture so that it might fit their self-centered desires. They would have only a superficial assent to religiosity as long as it fit their own ways. They would be selective in choosing what to adhere to and what to avoid. Only half truths, misrepresentations, and conjectures would be regarded, the rest disregarded.

3. They would *heap*, or pile up as many as possible, to themselves teachers, advisors, friends who would sympathize with them and support their way against God's way. Here again they would be choosey, selecting only the ones who would agree with them, discarding anyone who would disagree with them.

4. They would *turn away* their ears and hearts from the inconvenient truth of God's word, and would turn to convenient compromises and fables. They would even be bold enough to camouflage their rebelliousness with their supposed spirituality and their retarded religiosity.

Why Not Choose Life

We Will Serve the Lord

Joshua, Moses' courageous successor, made an impassioned appeal to the Israelites in the form of his last will and testament. He appealed to them to freely choose, but to choose to follow his example of serving God. He entreated them to "fear the Lord, serve Him in sincerity and in truth, and put away the gods which your fathers served . . ." Then he asked them to "choose for yourselves this day whom you will serve . . . But as for me and my house, we will serve the Lord" (Josh. 24:14, 15). In essence, this is what Joshua was saying to them: you may freely choose whom to serve, but I encourage you to choose right and serve God with me. If you decide to serve Him, He will bless you; but if you decide not to serve Him, He will forsake you. "If you forsake the Lord and serve foreign gods, then He will turn and do you harm and consume you, after He has done you good" (24:20).

"The command to serve the Lord does not preclude choice at all. Any service that is not voluntary is useless. God sets before men life and death and urges them to choose life, but He does not interfere with their contrary choice, nor does He protect them from its natural results." (*The SDA Bible Commentary*, vol. 2, p. 296). If we knowingly insist on making the wrong choice, then God lets us go our way, vulnerable to the evil consequences of our rebellion. Some believe that God's great love covers and excuses sin in His people, and does not allow Him to discipline them in their rebellion. But this is not true according to His reliable word. Notwithstanding our finite human opinions, we are to cling to God's sure and eternal word.

"But in all His dealings with His creatures God has maintained the principles of righteousness by revealing sin in its true character–by demonstrating that its sure result is misery and

183

death. The *unconditional pardon of sin never has been, and never will be.* Such [unconditional] pardon would show the *abandonment* of the principles of righteousness, which are the very foundation of the government of God. It would fill the unfallen universe with *consternation.* God has faithfully pointed out the results of sin, and if these warnings were not true, how could we be sure that His promises would be fulfilled? That *so-called benevolence* which would set aside justice is *not benevolence but weakness*" (*Patriarchs and Prophets*, p. 522; italics supplied). Earlier in this book, Ellen White referred to such mistaken notions about God's dealings as "mistaken kindness" resulting in "presumptuous rebellion."

Who Is on the Lord's Side?

Elijah the prophet who was translated to glory in fiery chariots, and who appeared with Moses on the Mount of Transfiguration, incessantly battled the forces of evil lurking all around him. The nation was in rebellion against God, with idolatry rampant under the influential leadership of eight hundred and fifty false prophets of Baal and Asherah. There were hundreds of false prophets, clearly showing the vast extent of their rebellious idolatry. But the crucial time for decision had come in this grave spiritual crisis. Like Moses, he was jealous for God's honor, and called for a decisive decision about God.

In the case of Moses, it was the wanton worship of the golden calf; and in the case of Elijah, it was the massive worship of Baal. Moses, in his righteous indignation, cried out: "Whoever is on the Lord's side–come to me!" (Ex. 32:26). And Elijah sounded the battle cry: "How long will you falter between two opinions? If the Lord is God, follow Him; but if Baal, follow him" (1 Kings 18:21). Why are you wavering and lukewarm toward declaring yourselves for God? Then there is the conditional: "If the Lord is God." But the Lord is indeed God, and there is absolutely no reason not to decide to follow Him. "But if Baal [is God]." Of course Baal is not God, so by all means choose not to follow him.

However, the reaction of the people was still doubtful: "But the people answered him not a word." You notice that when people are confronted with the truth they oppose, they often remain quiet. They have no moral courage or integrity to declare themselves loyal to it. "Not one in that vast assembly dare reveal loyalty to Jehovah. Like a dark cloud, *deception* and *blindness* had overspread Israel . . . *Not all at once* had this fatal apostasy closed about them . . . Each departure from right doing, each refusal to repent, had *deepened* their guilt and driven them farther from Heaven. And now, in this crisis, they persisted in refusing to take their stand for God" (*Prophets and Kings*, p. 147; italics supplied).

When we insist on going our way, unwilling to take our stand for God and His ways, then we end up fashioning our own idols of independence and insubordination. Our indecision toward God, and lukewarmness toward His truth is revolting to Him. In Revelation 3:16, our Lord becomes so nauseated with His lukewarm people that He is ready to "vomit" such out of His mouth. Commenting on the doubting and disloyal people of Elijah's day, Ellen White penned these strong words: "The Lord *abhors indifference and disloyalty* in a time of crisis in His work. The whole universe is watching with inexpressible interest the closing scenes of the great controversy . . . What can be of more importance to them than that they be loyal to the God of heaven?" (*Ibid.*, p. 148; italics supplied).

The prophet Ezekiel, suffering for God's wayward people, calls them to choose repentance over rebellion. He conveys

Christ's Way to Restoration

God's impassioned pleading with them to return to Him and live. "Say to them: 'As I live,' says the Lord God, 'I have no pleasure in the death of the wicked, but that the wicked turn from his way and live. Turn, turn from your evil ways! For why should you die, O house of Israel?'" (Ezek. 33:11). It is God's displeasure for us to disobey and die, and it is His pleasure for us to obey and live. See how earnestly emphatic He is when He twice pleads with them to "turn, turn" back to Him. Then He appeals in His persuasive way to their logic and common sense: "why should you die?" It is baffling, it makes no logical sense, it is needless to decide to die! With God giving all in giving His Son, why in the world would anyone choose death! By no means should we let Satan, the author of deception and death, put his blindfold on our eyes and hearts, enticing us to choose foolishness and death.

The Plea of Peter and Paul

The apostle Peter, in considering the coming collapse of this world, challenges us to live holy and godly lives. He clinches his point with this appeal: "Therefore, beloved, looking forward to these things, be diligent to be found by Him in peace, without spot and blameless" (2 Pet. 3:14). God is not neutral here, for in His heart He encourages us to choose Him and live holy for Him. He urges us to live His life and be ready for the soon coming of His Son. This is the manner of persons He ardently desires us to be. Why wouldn't we want to be such persons, considering the dissolution of this old world! It should not be business as usual, for the coming of the Lord is at hand. Why on earth should we invest more in this passing world, and less in the coming new world? It should be the exact opposite. Christ, in His great love for us, does not want us to just make a choice, but to make the right and smart choice of preparing for the end.

Why Not Choose Life

Paul tells us, as Christ's representatives, what our sacred responsibility is toward the lost. He urges us to persuade people to be reconciled to God. He does not use free choice as an excuse for neutrality, but as an impetus to make the right decision. Notice the urgent and compelling way he challenges us in 2 Corinthians 5:20. "Now then, we are ambassadors for Christ, as though God were pleading through us: we implore you on Christ's behalf, be reconciled to God." God does not just give people a choice to be reconciled to Him or not, but He *pleads* with them through us to be reconciled. Likewise, we too *implore* them on Christ's behalf to be reconciled. Tell me, what stronger words could Paul have employed to convey God's deliberate and determined desire to persuade us to make the right choice of coming to Him!

Either Hot or Cold

The glorified Lord, through John the Revelator, gives a clear picture of the conditionality of salvation for us today. Yes, He wants us to decide to either be hot or cold, but He desires even more that we be zealous for Him. Yes, free choice but the right choice to contritely repent and change our minds to be zealous for Jesus. Because of Christ's great love for us, we mourn our wrong ways, decide to open the our hearts to Him, and thus become zealous for Him.

Now, let us attentively hear His knock and listen responsively to His words: "As many as I love, I rebuke and chasten. Therefore be zealous and repent. Behold, I stand at the door and knock. If anyone hears My voice and opens the door, I will come in to him and dine with him, and he with Me. To him who overcomes, I will grant to sit with Me on My throne, as I also overcame and sat down with My Father on His throne" (Rev. 3:19-21). In Christ's passionate plea to His lukewarm yet loved people, we find His warm affection calling them to repentance and restoration. Notice the several elements of this special appeal to us today:

1. Considering our lukewarm spiritual state, Christ is by no means indifferent. Although He always respects our free choice, yet His strong love and warm affection compels Him to fight for His own.

2. His way of fiercely fighting for us is to lovingly rebuke and chastise us. We often associate the discipline of rebuke and chastisement with something negative, certainly not with love. But the opposite is true. Christ cares tremendously about us. In His loving-kindness He rebukes us in order to prick our consciences and convict our hearts to truly repent and be zealous. The wise man affirms this: "My son, do not despise the chastening of the Lord, nor detest His correction; for whom the Lord loves He corrects, just as a father the son in whom he delights" (Prov. 3:11, 12).

3. Christ is on a mission of mercy to rescue us, if we are willing, from our bad choices. He backs up His words with action: standing at the door, knocking with His hand, and speaking with His voice.

4. He wants us to know for sure that He means business. He is not there passively knocking and speaking just for the fun of it, and then quickly running off. No, not at all. He is determined to linger longer at the door of our lukewarm hearts, hoping against hope to be invited in. He is not just knocking but also calling our name, not in a rush to leave but to give us every incentive to decide for the right and open the door.

5. In the middle of Christ's exhortation we find the conditional factor of the "if" in our free choice: "If anyone hears My voice and opens the door . . ." (v. 20). Christ, no matter how

much He desires to come in, respects our choice of opening or not opening the door. He gives us every opportunity and every incentive, with all His persuasion, to choose to open. Yet He leaves it up to us to decide.

6. He wants us to overcome as He overcame, and to sit with Him on His throne. To triumph over our lukewarmness and become zealous for Him. It is interesting that the word "zealous" in Greek comes from the same root as the word *zestos*, which means "hot." Such *zestos* experience is not self-generated, but inspired by humble contrition, love, and loyalty to Christ.

7. Finally, the great and eternal reward Christ offers us when we choose to open our hearts to Him. He will fellowship with us here as cherished friends, feast with us in heaven as His beloved family, and sit with Him on His throne as majestic royalty.

A Knock and a Voice

How could we ever miss out on all the awesome blessings Christ has prepared for us to enjoy! How could we be so self-absorbed that we let Him continue to wait and wait, inattentive to His knock and deaf to His call! Years ago, as a carryover from my old culture, I would not only knock at a friend's door, but I would *also* call his name out to let him know that I really wanted to see him. But early in our marriage, my wife reminded me that in this country you just knock, and if there is no answer you leave, and that is it. In this culture it is not proper to persist this way, she said. But Jesus persists in knocking, talking, and walking back and forth, not wanting to leave, and watching for any sign of response on our part.

Please listen with your heart to this urgent appeal: "The Savior is waiting to enter your heart, why don't you let Him come in? There's nothing in this world to keep you apart, what is your

Christ's Way to Restoration

answer to Him? Time after time He has waited before, and now He is waiting again, to see if you're willing to open the door: O how He wants to come in." O my reader friend, do you hear His incessant gentle knock? Are you listening to His still small voice convicting your heart? Why not use your freedom of choice to never close your heart, but to ever open it to Him?

Discussion Questions

1. There is an emphasis today on unconditional pardon and approval granted by an unconditional God. Read Isaiah 55:6, 7, and then Isaiah 59:1, 2. Do you think God, His pardon, and approval are conditional or unconditional? Why or why not? What other texts can you find to support your answer?

2. Ellen White said that presuming upon God's mercy can exhaust it, for there is a limit to his forbearance. How do you understand this, considering that God's grace and forbearance are abundant?

3. There are those who bless themselves whom God has not blessed, and there are those who pray for God to approve their wayward ways. How would you describe such an attitude? What do you think is the cause of it? (See Deut. 29:18-20).

4. King Saul decided to sacrifice to God rather than obey Him. He camouflaged his lack of true spirituality with religious formality. How can we avoid such a pitfall? In what ways are we similar to Saul in this regard?

5. Why do we sometimes encourage people to make a decision merely for the sake of making one, rather than helping them make the right decision? Remember that although God respects our freedom of choice to make decisions, He is deliberate in urging us to make the right decisions.

Why Not Choose Life

6. Joshua said: "But as for me and my house, we will serve the Lord" (Josh. 24:15). What thoughts does this testimony stir in our hearts? How do we avoid making wrong decisions because of peer pressure? How do we stand firmly for the truth regardless of who follows us or who does not? Remember what Jesus said to Peter, "What is that to you? You follow Me" (Jn. 21:22).

7. When Elijah appealed to the apostate children of Israel to return to their true God, they were speechless. Why do you think they reacted in this manner? Contemplate this statement to learn that their spiritual depravity was something gradual: "Each departure from right doing, each refusal to repent, had deepened their guilt and driven them farther from Heaven" (*Prophets and Kings*, p. 147).

8. Read about the lukewarm Laodiceans in Revelation 3:14-22. How do we view Christ's actions when He loves us, yet chastises and rebukes us? Or when He urges us to repent and be zealous? Notice that such chastisement is expressed in the context of His great hope for us: fellowship with us here, overcoming, and sitting with Him on His throne.

9. Jesus does not tolerate neutrality or appeasement. What does this tell us about His character, and the ways He deals with us? How is this helpful to us in our spiritual growth?

10. Jesus not only stands at the door of our heart, but He knocks, He waits, and He speaks. What does this tell you about His ardent desire and deliberate intentionality to reach us? He is waiting now to see if we are willing to open our hearts to Him. Are we hearing His incessant knock? Are we listening to His pleading voice? He greatly desires to come in! Why not open our hearts now and let Him in?

Conclusion

In this brief conclusion, I would like to share with you a personal experience to illustrate how staying the course with Jesus leads us to full restoration. Our Lord's loving plan is that we adhere to His way not our way, to become Christlike not self-like, to freely choose the right, and to relinquish our wilfulness and to embrace His will.

I will entitle this experience, "If you stick with me, you'll make it." This encouraging counsel was given to me by a faithful and loyal friend, and more importantly a friend faithful and loyal to Jesus. Years ago he and I were jogging partners, thanks to his consistent encouragement. Being stronger and more fit than me, he would assuringly say: "If I you stick with me, you'll make it." Whenever I would be tempted to slack off, or whenever I would get tired, his confident words would boost my spirit and spur me on my way. For many months we enjoyed jogging together.

One morning he asked me to go cycling with him. I knew he was a skilled and strong cyclist, tempered by years of experience. When I expressed doubt about my cycling abilities, he would repeat the same words: "If you stick with me, you'll make it." Our destination was a nearby lake, several miles away. As we proceeded on our way down the road, the cycling was no problem for me, thanks to the road being level or downhill. The trip was smooth and enjoyable.

Conclusion

On the way back, it was a different story. The road was now uphill in several stretches, as I struggled using my lower gears to keep going. One steep stretch proved too much for me as I put my bicycle in its lowest gear, zigzagging my way forward. In the middle of that hill, I placed my full weight on the pedals but to no avail. The bicycle came to an abrupt halt, and I just could not budge, no matter how hard I tried. With ease, my friend was breezing his way ahead of me. But when he noticed that I stopped in mid course, he came back saying, "If you stick with me, you'll make it."

Realizing that my energy was totally spent, he lined up his bicycle next to mine, and told me to steer my bicycle but not to pedal with my exhausted legs. Then he placed his strong hand behind my bicycle seat, and with the other hand he steered his bike. To my total amazement, he started pedaling his bicycle, pulling me along with him up the hill! I easily steered as He did all the arduous work of pushing us both forward. At the top of the hill, the road became level again, so he let me pedal. As we bicycled leisurely side by side, he looked at me and said: "I told you, didn't I, that if you stick with me, you'll make it."

My friend showed me a glimpse of Jesus. Our Savior and Lord is our most loving and loyal Friend, and He is cycling life's challenging journey with us. We are homeward bound–from His kingdom of grace to His kingdom of glory. In this adventurous journey, there are ups and downs, trials and triumphs, but He always remains in control. Watch His spiritual muscles flex for you and me, enabling us to move forward with Him. Hear His encouraging voice sound loud and clear: "If you stick with Me, you'll make it!" All He asks of us is to do what we can, to do our best with His best. Why not choose right now to love and trust Him with all our hearts and obey Him with all our souls? He wants us to submit to Him in order to fashion us as chosen and precious vessels for His glorious kingdom. Lovingly and loyally let us stick with Him, no matter what may happen, until the very end.

Tell me, my good friend, on this journey together, why not be found cycling with Jesus until He comes.

Christ's Way to Pray

HOW CHRIST PRAYS FOR US AND WITH US

PHILIP G. SAMAAN

Author of *Christ's Way to Spiritual Growth, Christ's Way of Reaching People,* and *Christ's Way of Making Disciples*

A Christ-centered approach to prayer. It shows how Christ is our mighty prayer warrior in praying for us and with us, thus giving our prayer life confidence and efficacy. When we pray in faith Jesus is there to embrace us with His loving human arm, and with His divine arm to connect us with the Throne.

Christ's Way of Reaching People

Philip G. Samaan

The Fine Art of Relational Witnessing

The focus is on the fine art of relational witnessing. It presents the six steps of Christ's way of reaching people, and how we may successfully model such steps in our daily lives. The book is punctuated with numerous illustrations and experiences to make it easy to apply.

Christ's Way to Spiritual Growth

Author of *Christ's Way of Reaching People*

Philip G. Samaan

Christian spirituality is the dynamic process of becoming Christlike. The emphasis in this book is on modeling Christ's example of true spirituality in such a way that people who interact with us take notice that we have been with Jesus.

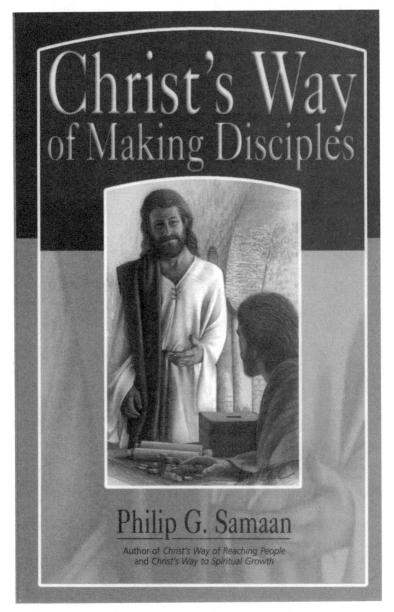

Christ's Way
of Making Disciples

Philip G. Samaan

Author of *Christ's Way of Reaching People*
and *Christ's Way to Spiritual Growth*

The urgent need of the church today is not merely to win converts, but to reproduce and multiply fruitful disciples. This book explores the dynamic process and progressive steps of Christ's approach of transforming us and others into fruit-bearing disciples.

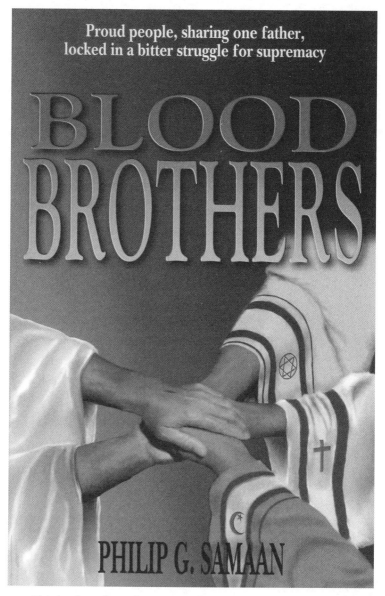

Proud people, sharing one father,
locked in a bitter struggle for supremacy

BLOOD BROTHERS

PHILIP G. SAMAAN

This book explores the common heritage that binds the three great monotheistic religions together, namely Judaism, Christianity, and Islam. It explains the bitter rivalry among these blood brothers; and presents our Elder Blood Brother Jesus Christ as the only real solution. It also helps Western minds understand the real issues in this ancient family feud.